Artist Profiles

Columbus, OH

Photo Credits

3 ©Anthony Barboza/Black Images; 4 Complimentary Paul Baliker; 5 ©David Woo; 6 ©Conde Nast Archive/Corbis; 7 Complimentary Lee Udall Bennion; 8 ©AP/Wide World Photos; 9 ©Annie O'Neill; 10 ©Reuters/Corbis-Bettmann; 11 Complimentary Paul Brach; 12 ©Bettmann/Corbis; 13 Complimentary Nathaniel Bustion; 14 ©Dominique Berretty/Black Star; 15 Laura Platt Winfrey/Woodfin Camp & Associates; 16 ©Scala/Art Resource, NY; 17 ©Erich Lessing/Art Resource, NY; 18 ©Getty Images; 19 ©Bryson John/Corbis Sygma; 20 ©Royal Library, Turin, Italy. Scala/Art Resource, NY; 21 ©French Cultural Services/Laurie Platt Winfrey/Woodfin Camp & Associates; 22 ©Hulton-Deutsch Collection/Corbis; 23 Complimentary Randy Ellett; 24 ©Archivo Iconografico, S.A./Corbis; 25 ©Nina Howell Starr/Photo Researchers; 26 ©Bettmann/Corbis; 27 ©Paul Almasy/Corbis; 28 ©Bettmann/Corbis; 29 ©George W. Hart; 30 ©National Portrait Gallery, Smithsonian Institution/Art Resource, NY; 31 Helen Borch Bartlett Memorial Collection, 1926.212 Photograph by Bob Hashimoto. Image © The Art Institute of Chicago; 32 ©Getty Images; 33 ©Bettmann/Corbis; 34 ©Nevada Historical Society; 35 National Gallery of Art, Washington D.C. Gift of Otto and Franziska Kallir with the help of the Carol and Edwin Gaines Fullinwider Fund; 36 Complimentary Susan Le Van; 37 Complimentary Christina Lemon; 38 ©Fred Lyon Pictures; 39 ©Prestel-Verlag; 40 ©UPI/Corbis-Bettmann; 41 ©Burstein Collection/Corbis; 42 Complimentary Cristina Iglesias; 43 ©Oscar White/Corbis; 44 ©Bettmann/Corbis; 45 ©Getty Images; 46 ©Carl Solway Gallery, Cincinnati, Ohio, Photographer: J.M. Cockerill; 47 ©Giraudon/Art Resource, NY; 48 ©Bettmann/Corbis; 40 Courtesy, Museum of Fine Arts, Boston; 50 Complimentary Rosalind Ragans; 51 ©Bettmann/Corbis; 52 Complimentary Timothy Rose; 53 Collection of the Modern Art Museum of Fort Worth, Museum Purchase, Sid W. Richardson Foundation Endowment Fund and an Anonymous Donor; 54 ©Art Resource, NY; 55 Complimentary Julia Russell; 56 ©Bettmann/Corbis; 57 ©Suzanne Opton/Courtesy Steinbaum Krauss Gallery; 58 ©AKG London; 59 ©Christopher Felver/Corbis; 60 Amon Carter Museum, Fort Worth, Texas. 1999.33.E; 61 ©Daniel Budnik; 62 ©Timothy Greenfield-Sanders; 63 ©The William E. Finch, Jr. Archives, The Historical Society of the Town of Greenwich; 64 ©Metropolitan Museum of Art, NY, Bequest of Miss Adelaide Milton de Groot 91876-1967), 1967 (67.187.70a); 65 ©Kevin Fleming/Corbis; 66 Complimentary John Warren; 67 ©Bettmann/Corbis; 69 The Metropolitan Museum of Art, Munsey Fund, 1932. Photography ©1991 The Metropolitan Museum of Art; 70 Collection American Folk Art Museum, New York. Gift of Jackie and Stanley Schneider. 1980.31.2. Photo Matt Hoebermann; 71 Photograph ©Frank Fortune; 72 Dallas Museum of Art, Dallas, Texas; 73 Dallas Museum of Art, Dallas, Texas; 74 Complimentary Rosalind Ragans; 75 Cleveland Museum of Art, Cleveland, Ohio; 76 North Carolina Museum of Art, Purchased with funds provided through a bequest from Lucile E. Moorman; 77 Complimentary Rosalind Ragans; 78 Seattle Art Museum, Gift of John H. Hauberg. Photograph by Paul Macapia; 79 St. Louis Museum of Art. Museum Shop Fund; 80 International Folk Art Foundation Collection. Museum of International Folk Art. Santa Fe, New Mexico. Photo by: Pat Pollard; 81 ©Ferrell McCollough/SuperStock; 82 Dallas Museum of Art, the Patsy R. and Raymond D. Nasher Collection of Maya Textiles from Guatemala, gift of Patsy R. and Raymond D. Nasher.

SRAonline.com

Copyright © 2005 by SRA/McGraw-Hill.

All rights reserved. Except as permitted under the United States Copyright Act, no part of this publication may be reproduced or distributed in any form or by any means, or stored in a database or retrieval system, without the prior written permission of the publisher, unless otherwise indicated.

Send all inquiries to:
SRA/McGraw-Hill
8787 Orion Place
Columbus, OH 43240-4027

Printed in the United States of America.

ISBN 0-07-601839-3

1 2 3 4 5 6 7 8 9 DBH 08 07 06 05 04

Table of Contents

Andrews, Benny 3
Baliker, Paul A. 4
Bates, David 5
Bellows, George 6
Bennion, Lee 7
Bishop, Isabel 8
Blanco, Teadora 9
Botero, Fernando 10
Brach, Paul 11
Braque, Georges 12
Bustion, Nathaniel 13
Calder, Alexander 14
Cassatt, Mary 15
Cézanne, Paul 16
Chardin, Jean-Baptiste Simeon 17
Copley, John Singleton 18
Dalí, Salvador 19
da Vinci, Leonardo 20
Derain, André 21
Eiffel, Gustave 22
Ellett, Randy 23
Ensor, James 24
Evans, Minnie 25
Gauguin, Paul 26
Giacometti, Alberto 27
Grandma Moses 28
Hart, George W. 29
Hartley, Marsden 30
Hodler, Ferdinand 31
Hokusai, Katsushika 32
Kahlo, Frida 33
Keyser, Louisa (Dat So La Lee) 34
Klimt, Gustav 35
LeVan, Susan 36
Lemon, Christina 37
MacDonald-Wright, Stanton 38
Marc, Franz 39
Matisse, Henri 40
Munch, Edvard 41
Muñoz, Juan 42

Neel, Alice 43
Nevelson, Louise 44
O'Keeffe, Georgia 45
Paik, Nam June 46
Pannini, Giovanni Paolo 47
Picasso, Pablo 48
Powers, Harriet 49
Ragans, Rosalind 50
Renoir, Pierre-Auguste 51
Rose, Timothy 52
Rothenberg, Susan 53
Rousseau, Henri 54
Russell, Julia 55
Safdie, Moshe 56
Schapiro, Miriam 57
Schmidt-Rottluff, Karl 58
Segal, George 59
Sharp, William 60
Smith, David 61
Thiebaud, Wayne 62
Twachtman, John Henry 63
van Gogh, Vincent 64
van Rijn, Rembrandt 65
Warren, John 66
Weber, Max 67
Akrafokonmu (Soul Discs) 68
Armor of George Clifford 69
Bull's Eye Quilt 70
Carved Animals 71
Ceremonial Hanging 72
Ceremonial Skirt 73
Coming of Age Hat 74
Dancing Lady 75
Egungun from Ogbomoso 76
Face Jugs 77
Face Mask of K̲umugwe' 78
King's Crown 79
Quilt 80
United States Capitol 81
Woman's Headcloth 82

• Artist Profile •

Benny Andrews
b. 1930

Benny Andrews (ben´ ē an´ drūz) was born in rural Georgia during the Great Depression. His parents were farmers. They raised ten children. Andrews grew up watching his father George paint pictures on every available surface. Benny himself scratched pictures in the dirt with sticks. After high school, he served in the United States Air Force. At the time, Georgia did not permit African American students to attend its art schools. A federal law forced the state to pay part of Andrews's tuition to an out-of-state school. Andrews was able to earn a degree at the Art Institute of Chicago. But even there, the work of African American students was not included in student shows. After a long struggle, Andrews finally achieved recognition. His art now hangs in museums around the world, and he has taught and lectured at colleges across the nation.

About Art History
During the 1960s, Andrews led protests to have the art of African Americans exhibited. In 1982, he went to work for the National Endowment for the Arts, where he set up programs to help minority artists. He made sure they had many opportunities to show their work.

About the Artwork
Andrews's art, such as his *Southland Series,* focuses on people and places that were part of his southern upbringing. *Daydreams of a Young Boy* was inspired by his childhood desire to become a cowboy.

About the Media
Andrews is most recognized for his pen and ink drawings. In one of his early paintings, *Janitors at Rest,* he added paper towels and bathroom tissue. Since then he has often combined oils and collage.

About the Technique
Andrews often uses a neutral background to focus attention on his subject. He also uses actual articles in his paintings, such as a real blacksmith's apron in *The Blacksmith.*

Artist Profile

Paul Baliker
b. 1970

Paul Baliker (pôl bä´ li kər) created his first sculpture at the age of eight. To earn money during his college years, he collected driftwood from beaches and rivers and whittled simple images into it. Since then sculpting has been his passion and livelihood. Baliker is a self-taught artist, and his interest in nature has drawn him to the water. He can often be found fishing or surfing. Spending so much time near the water has provided him with an intense respect for nature.

About Art History

National attention was focused on Baliker's work when the PBS special *For the Love of Manatees* aired. The special was filmed around the creation of his life-size sculpture of a manatee and calf, *Wellspring*. The program was created to help build the public's understanding of manatees. It also increased public awareness of both Baliker's talent and his dedication to the relationship of people to their environment.

About the Artwork

Baliker's life-size wood sculpture *Evolution* is housed in New York's Empire State Building. Other works appear in Florida's Daytona International Airport, the Orange County Convention Center, and in sculpture gardens in Michigan and Oklahoma.

About the Media

Baliker sculpts in wood and also has sculptures cast in bronze.

About the Technique

Baliker spends hours researching and often observes his subjects before he begins to create a sculpture. All of his sculptures are initially carved in wood. If a piece is to be cast in bronze, he first creates a rubber mold. The bronze work, created using the lost wax process, is completed at a foundry where he oversees the work.

UNIT 1 • Lesson 4

Artist Profile

David Bates
b. 1952

David Bates (dā´ vid bātz) was born in Goshen, Indiana. He received a bachelor of fine arts degree from Southern Methodist University (SMU) in Dallas, Texas. He then became part of the Whitney Museum's independent study program and later returned to SMU to complete his master of fine arts degree.

About Art History
Bates went to New York where he spent a year working with artist Red Grooms. During his time there, Bates was exposed to many personalities, influences, and works of art. Since that time he has used many different styles and media, and his work shows the influence of folk and wildlife art.

About the Artwork
Bates is known for his offbeat, rural subject matter. He has exhibited widely across the United States, and his work is part of the collections of several major museums, including the Metropolitan Museum of Art, Whitney Museum of Art, San Francisco Museum of Modern Art, Dallas Museum of Art, and Museum of Fine Arts, Houston. Bates's work has been described as a form of *regionalism*, because his works are often about specific geographical and cultural subjects.

About the Media
Bates creates prints, paintings, and sculptures. He frequently uses oils for his paintings and casts his sculptures in bronze.

About the Technique
Bates paints in a style reminiscent of the folk artists whose work he admires and collects. Many of Bates's figures are depicted in a larger-than-life manner. He uses dense contrasting colors and texture in his artwork to create a three-dimensional aspect.

Artist Profile

George Bellows
1882–1925

George Bellows (jôrj bel´ lōz), a native of Columbus, Ohio, showed an early talent for both drawing and athletics. After several years at The Ohio State University, where he made sketches for the yearbook and the student newspaper, Bellows left college to play semiprofessional baseball. His baseball earnings, plus the sale of several drawings enabled him to go to New York and study art. He lived in an apartment across the street from Sharkey's, a prizefighting club that became the setting of his famous painting *Stag at Sharkey's*. Restless and ambitious, he was always ready to try new projects and techniques. By the time he was 28, he was selling his paintings, and later his lithographs, to top collectors. Bellows married his college sweetheart and had two daughters. He died suddenly at age 42 of a ruptured appendix.

About Art History

Bellows is part of the ashcan school of painting. At the New York School of Art he studied under Robert Henri, who sent his students into the street to observe reality and beauty in the urban scene. Not interested in studying art in France or Italy, Bellows was an American realist painter.

About the Artwork

In his short life, Bellows managed to finish more than 600 oil paintings and thousands of drawings and lithographs. Some of his art focused on the violence in boxing. *Both Members of the Club* shows two fierce, sweaty, bloody boxers. He also painted sensitive portraits, and seascapes and cityscapes full of movement and energy.

About the Media

Bellows most often worked in oils.

About the Technique

Bellows's early paintings were marked by slashing brushstrokes and had a dark, smoky look that captured the mood of illegal prizefighting clubs. Later in his career he used a geometric formula to compose his human figures. Some thought this approach took the life out of his paintings.

Artist Profile

Lee Bennion
b. 1956

Lee Bennion (lē ben´ yən) was born in Merced, California, in 1956. She moved to Utah in 1974 to study art at Brigham Young University. Two years later she moved with her ceramicist husband to Spring City, a rural Utah town with a thriving art community. Lee's family is very important to her, as are her church and community, and the subject matter of her paintings revolve around them. In 1983, Bennion returned to Brigham Young University, where she earned her master of fine arts degree in painting. The environment is another important part of Bennion's life, and she wants to see the wilderness of the American Southwest preserved. She spends much of her time outdoors and incorporates the brilliant colors of her surroundings into her landscape paintings. Bennion currently lives and works Spring City.

About Art History

Bennion's spirituality is reflected in her work. She often includes Christian symbolism in her colorful paintings and seeks to portray not just the factual representation of her subjects, but their emotions as well. She has received numerous awards and frequently participates in workshops for artists, students and educators. Bennion sells her work through galleries in Salt Lake City, Utah, and Palm Springs, California, and many private collections and museums own her work.

About the Artwork

Form, color, and feeling are the primary focuses of Bennion's paintings. In her portraits, Bennion's bright, elongated figures gaze directly at the viewer. In her 1992 piece *Snow Queen: Portrait of Adah*, Bennion's young daughter Adah stands in front of a large window with her foot propped against the window's side and a troll doll in her hand. Adah's elongated body contrasts with the window's geometric shapes, and the snow falling outside mirrors the paper snowflakes in the window. When Bennion created this painting she was fully occupied with her family and home, and she spent the majority of her days indoors. The interior portion of this painting represents her life at the time and the window suggests change and future possibilities.

About the Media

Lee Bennion paints in oils on canvas.

About the Technique

Bennion sketches and paints from a model. Oil paints dry slowly, which allows her to rework an image or color for a longer period of time. She uses texture, and typically paints thin layers before thick layers, as thick layers will not dry if covered with additional paint.

Artist Profile

Isabel Bishop
1902–1988

Isabel Bishop (iz´ a bel bish´ əp) was born in Cincinnati, Ohio. A year later, her family moved to a run-down neighborhood in Detroit, Michigan, where her father was employed as the principal of a nearby high school. Her parents didn't think the neighborhood children made good playmates, so Bishop spent much of her time alone. She graduated from high school at age 15 and then studied art. She moved to New York City, where she continued to study art and began exhibiting her work. She loved to paint the people in Union Square.

Bishop married in 1934, moved to the suburbs, and had a son. She commuted to her studio on the Square every day for 40 years. Looking down from her studio in an office building, she watched the people below as she worked. During her life, Bishop won many awards and honors. Her paintings hang in museums across the nation.

About Art History

Bishop's style was influenced by the Baroque period and especially the work of Peter Paul Rubens. She liked the way he used layers of washes as an underpainting and then added glazes over the painting to create a sense of movement. Bishop's early work was "real beyond reality." It gradually gained an abstract cubist quality as she began to emphasize the patterns she saw in the architecture, colors, and shadows of Union Square.

About the Artwork

Bishop created paintings, drawings, and prints. She is best known for her pictures of Union Square, such as *On the Street*. Sometimes called an "urban realist," she painted the shoppers and workers in the square.

About the Media

Bishop painted in oils over tempera and created etchings in aquatint.

About the Technique

Toward the end of her career, Bishop added transparent veils of color and networks of dots and lines to her paintings. She portrayed people as nearly transparent; they seemed to be moving in a mist, contributing to the overall abstract quality.

Artist Profile

Teodora Blanco
1928–1980

Teodora Blanco (tā´ ō dôr ä blän´ kō) was born in a poor village in Mexico where little girls were required to learn to make pots. Their plain but useful pots were sold to help support the family. Unlike many of her playmates, Blanco loved to work with clay. When she went to the market to sell her pots, she also stopped at the museum to study the artwork there. In time, she began to decorate her pots with figures. Blanco's unique pots sold well, so she was encouraged to experiment with her figures.

As she became a recognized artist, Blanco took an active role in her community, helping families in need as well as encouraging young potters. Now three of her five children carry on the family pottery tradition. As they fill orders sent in from around the world, they work in the style their mother developed. Nelson Rockefeller was one of Blanco's admirers and bought her work for museum collections.

About Art History

As a self-taught artist Blanco began sculpting with clay in a simple folk art style. One early example is *Market Woman,* which shows a native woman carrying pots she hopes to sell. Gradually Blanco shifted to an elaborate rococo style, such as *Kangaroo Rat,* which shows a sculpture of a figure covered with floral designs.

About the Artwork

Blanco expressed the myths and beliefs of her heritage in clay. She created human and animal figures as spirits to protect people. She often combined human and animal characteristics in one figure, which might be as tall as 30 inches. Blanco covered many of her figures with flowers as symbols of fertility, which was so important to families that depend on farming. She also created scenes of animals playing musical instruments, reminiscent of musicians in her village.

About the Media

Blanco worked entirely with clay.

About the Technique

Blanco, like her children today, created her pots and figures on a covered porch behind her simple home. She fired them in a homemade kiln and stored them in huts with thatched roofs.

Artist Profile

Fernando Botero
b. 1932

As a young man, this Colombian spent two years learning to be a matador. Fernando Botero (fer nän´ dō bōtā´ rō) changed his career plans and studied art in Colombia, Spain, France, and Italy. During this time, Botero had several exhibitions, but received little praise for his work—and fewer sales. After he began painting in a rounded style in 1956, his pictures sold well. By 1958, he was Colombia's most famous young artist. In 1960, he opened a studio in New York City. In 1973, he moved to Paris and began sculpting. He has married twice and has four children.

About Art History

In his early years, Botero was influenced by modern French and Spanish painters, along with the Renaissance masters. At one time he was expelled from a conservative art school for praising Picasso. In time, he settled on his own style, which features rounded figures.

About the Artwork

Botero draws portraits of individuals and groups. Much of his work shows the influence of his South American background, such as its food, music, religion, and architecture. Some characters appear again and again in his work, such as a Colombian man with a thin mustache. His sculptures range from human figures and animals to a giant coffeepot. Many pieces have the same rounded shapes he uses in his drawings. Some of Botero's work is serious and some is playful.

About the Media

Botero expresses his ideas in oils, pencil and charcoal drawings, watercolors, and bronze and marble sculptures.

About the Technique

Botero sometimes does quick sketches before beginning an oil painting. Many of his drawings, however, are finished works of art. He completes some in charcoal on canvas, such as *A Family*. For other drawings, he uses a thick pencil but no shading. When sculpting, Botero begins by making a sketch or a clay model. Then a workshop produces a plaster model for him, and Botero decides whether to have technicians carve the finished product in marble or cast it in bronze.

Artist Profile

Paul Brach
b. 1924

Paul Brach (pôl bräk) was born and raised in New York City. Even though Brach grew up during the Great Depression, his family was not hit hard financially, and he was afforded a privileged education. As a teenager he spent his summers working on ranches in Arizona. He developed an appreciation for the freedom and space of the West, and evidence of this experience continues to appear in his paintings. He attended the University of Iowa, one of the first schools to offer a degree in creative work. After serving in World War II, Paul returned to the United States and married Miriam Shapiro, a widely respected painter whom he had met in Iowa. Today, Brach lives in New York and continues to ride his horse every Sunday.

About Art History

Paul Brach's earlier work is painted in an abstract expressionist style. *Abstraction* dealt with simple, orderly compositions. *Expressionism* was a manipulation of formal or representational elements to convey intense feelings. Abstract expressionism originated as an art movement in the early 1940s and included a variety of styles, not all of which were abstract or expressionistic. Surrealism and cubism had a direct effect on many abstract expressionists, and color field painting, gesturalism, assemblage and graffiti emerged from its influence. Some of Brach's contemporaries included Roy Lichtenstein, Bob Rauschenberg, Bob Irwin, Ed Kienholz and Larry Bell.

About the Artwork

In the 1980s, Brach became interested in the patterns he saw in the Navajo blankets of America's Southwest. He created several paintings in which he combined the patterns of the blankets with the monumental landscapes in which the weavers live. *Chuska* is the name of a mountain range in the northeastern corner of the Navajo reservation in Arizona. The blanket that inspired the pattern in Brach's work *Chuska* is in Santa Fe.

About the Media

Brach works primarily in oils on canvas. *Chuska* was created with oil and gold leaf on canvas.

Artist Profile

Georges Braque
1882–1963

Georges Braque (zhorzh brak) was born in Argenteuil-sur-Seine, France. Helping his father, a house decorator, taught him much about painting. In 1900 he moved to Paris to study under a master decorator. He then spent several years painting at the Académie Humbert. Braque worked with Pablo Picasso in creating cubism, but after fighting in World War I, he ended his work with Picasso. His style constantly evolved until his death in 1963.

About Art History

Braque began painting in the impressionist style, but soon was attracted to fauvism—a style whose name comes from a French word for "wild beasts." Fauvists, such as Henri Matisse, tended to use colors in an intense and violent way. Braque's style took another turn when he met Pablo Picasso and saw his *Les Demoiselles d'Avignon*. Together Braque and Picasso worked to develop cubism, a style that shows the world from a number of different viewpoints.

About the Artwork

After meeting Picasso, Braque began to paint stark, abstract landscapes of geometric forms. As Braque and Picasso developed the cubist style, Braque began to incorporate collage into his paintings. His most abstract works of art during this time were filled with gray, brown, and black broken forms.

After 1917 Braque's work combined cubism with decorative, sensual elements, and by the end of his life he painted nature in a more realistic way.

About the Media

Braque was the first cubist to incorporate collages of pasted paper into his paintings. In addition to paintings, Braque created lithographs, sculptures, stained-glass windows, and jewelry designs. He also designed the sets for two ballets.

About the Technique

Braque and Picasso went through several developmental phases of cubism. During one of these phases, Braque tried to reduce natural forms to basic geometric shapes and show them on a two-dimensional plane. He glued bits of paper, sand, and sawdust into some of his paintings to create texture.

Artist Profile

Nathaniel Bustion
b. 1942

Nathaniel Bustion (nə than´ yəl bū tən) was born in Gadsden, Alabama, in 1942. He graduated from the Otis Art Institute where he received a master of fine arts degree. He also studied at the Belgium Antwerp Academy and attended several workshops at Ife University in Nigeria. Bustion's paintings, prints, and sculptures reflect his worldwide travels.

About Art History

Bustion is influenced by ancient African and Egyptian art. Many other artists have looked to cultures around the world for inspiration, for example Paul Gauguin moved from France to Tahiti so he could paint island imagery. A group of artists who call themselves symbolists followed Gauguin's artistic examples. Gustave Moreau and Odilon Redon were two other symbolists. Pablo Picasso's cubist movement was inspired by African and oceanic sculpture and masks.

About the Artwork

Bustion has created three series of works. His *Egyptian Mummies* is a bold series of symbolic prints showing Egyptian beliefs about the journey of the soul after death. The prints are geometric and abstract. The *African Masks* series focuses on African masks, faces, primitive patterns, and totems. Bustion's *Brownstone Series* is a collection of sculptures. They are long and tall like totem poles. On their surfaces Bustion combines ancient African imagery and geometric designs with multiple faces. These faces often blend together into one head-like structure.

About the Technique

In his stoneware sculptures Bustion builds forms by hand and then shapes them with sculpting tools. He covers the surfaces with glazes in a variety of colors. Bustion uses a casting process to make his bronze sculptures. His printmaking process is time consuming and difficult, because Bustion individualizes some of them using oil paints or airbrushing.

Artist Profile

Alexander Calder
1871–1945

Alexander Calder (a leg zan´ dər kôl´ dər) had a mother who painted, and both his father and grandfather were sculptors. Calder liked to make gadgets. He trained to be an engineer. Later he attended art school and worked as a commercial artist. In 1926, he moved to Paris, France, and began to experiment with making tiny circuses out of wood, cork, and wire. In 1931, he used his training as an engineer to create motor-driven sculptures. A year later he invented *mobiles*—sculptures that move in the wind.

Calder traveled to Europe, South America, and Asia with his wife and two daughters. He created works of art wherever he went. His work became very popular. It has appeared in many public buildings, including the Lincoln Center for the Performing Arts in New York City. He never named his work until it was installed. His last mobile, which remains untitled, hangs in the National Gallery of Art in Washington, D.C.

About Art History

Calder was the first artist known for creating mobiles. He also produced what he called *stabiles*. These sculptures look like mobiles, but do not move. Calder sometimes combined mobiles with stabiles. Much of Calder's work is abstract. For example, his sculpture *Hanging Spider* suggests a spider, but does not have eight legs. Calder's style was influenced by his friendship with the surrealist painters Joan Miró and Piet Mondrain.

About the Artwork

Calder meant for his sculptures to suggest movements and shapes from nature, such as clouds, leaves, or waves. Some of his works are very large. For example, a wire sculpture of a woman, *Spring*, is seven feet high.

About the Media

Calder created his mobiles and stabiles from wire and metal, balancing them carefully so they move in the slightest breeze. He also made drawings, paintings, prints, and stage sets.

About the Technique

Calder usually began a large sculpture by first creating a small-scale model. Then he directed the making of the final sculpture.

Artist Profile

Mary Cassatt
1845–1926

Mary Cassatt (merˊ ē kə satˊ) was born into an upper middle-class family in western Pennsylvania in 1884. She was enrolled at the Pennsylvania Academy of the Fine Arts from 1861 to 1865. She later studied in Paris, France, in the studios of Geróme and Couture. In 1874, she settled permanently in Paris, where she regularly submitted work to the yearly Salon exhibitions. The painter and sculptor Edgar Degas saw her work at the Salon and invited Cassatt to join the Impressionists in 1887. She was the only American ever to exhibit in the group's shows. During her lifetime, Cassatt's work was more popular in Europe than in the United States. In her spare time, she loved to entertain friends and ride her horses. As Cassatt got older her eyesight began to fail, and by 1914 she was unable to paint.

About Art History

An etching revival in France in 1862 was marked by the founding of the Societe des Aquafortistes (Society of Etchers). The leaders of this revival, Félix Bracquemond and Alfred Cadart, encouraged important painters of the day to make prints. Degas, Manet, Pissarro, and Cassatt were among those who made prints and experimented with graphic techniques.

About the Artwork

Cassatt is famous for painting mothers with their children, though she had no children of her own. Degas reportedly encouraged Cassatt to paint women and children. At the time few artists did so, except in religious scenes. Cassatt also painted quiet moments in the lives of women.

About the Media

Cassatt painted with oils. She also made many pastel and pencil drawings, as well as prints.

About the Technique

Cassatt mixed her colors directly on the canvas. Her compositions were strongly influenced by the asymmetrical arrangements of Japanese wood-block prints.

▲ **Paul Cézanne.** (French). *Self Portrait with Hat.* c. 1879

Oil on canvas. $44\frac{1}{2} \times 33$ inches (113 × 84 cm.) Kunstmuseum, Bern, Switzerland.

Artist Profile

Paul Cézanne
1839–1906

Paul Cézanne (paul sā zan´) was born in the south of France in Aix-en-Provence. He is often called the father of modern art. He loved to paint, but people did not like his work much—at least not during his lifetime. He had to beg gallery owners to show his work, and therefore he did not sell many paintings. He inherited money from his parents to pay his bills and buy his paints. He continued painting until a week before he died.

About Art History

Cézanne was a postimpressionist. He was greatly influenced by the painter Camille Pissarro. Pissarro introduced Cézanne to the new impressionist technique for capturing outdoor light. Cézanne combined impressionism with a formal instruction the impressionists had abandoned. He looked closely at things to find their basic forms and shapes. Cézanne painted cylinders, spheres, and cones to show these forms. Sometimes he changed the shapes he saw in nature to make his paintings more interesting. Picasso, Matisse, and other artists studied Cézanne's ideas.

About the Artwork

Cézanne painted landscapes, still lifes, and portraits. Many of his landscapes were of the countryside and mountains near his home. He developed a unique way of representing nature and objects in a highly creative and abstract fashion. Cézanne painted slowly, often taking several days to create a still life. One friend posed 115 times so Cézanne could finish his portrait.

About the Media

Cézanne worked in both oils and watercolors.

About the Technique

Cézanne used bright colors and bold brushstrokes, especially in the skies of his landscapes. He applied the paint in vertical and horizontal lines. He knew that cool colors seem to pull back and warm colors seem to go forward. Cézanne also used different shades of the same color to add shape to his subjects. His knowledge made his paintings seem three-dimensional.

Artist Profile

Jean-Baptiste Siméon Chardin
1699–1779

▲ **Jean-Baptiste Siméon Chardin.** (French). *Still Life with the Attributes of the Arts.* 1766.

Oil on canvas. 44 × 55 inches (111.76 × 139.7 cm.). Hermitage, St. Petersburg, Russia.

John Baptiste Siméon Chardin (zhä[n] ba tēst´ si´ mā´ ən shär dan´), a French painter of the eighteenth century, was born in Paris in 1699. His early artistic skills were self-taught, and he was strongly influenced by seventeenth-century painters like Metsu. After an independent beginning, Chardin attended the Royal Academy of Painting and Sculpture, and in the 1730s, painted scenes of Parisian bourgeois life. The majority of his paintings were commissioned or supported by wealthy aristocrats, including King Louis XV. Chardin was primarily a still-life painter, and he is still regarded as a master of realism and form.

About Art History

During Chardin's career, many of his contemporaries concentrated on painting dynamic historical subjects and rococo scenes, but he did not follow this trend. Instead Chardin focused on the simple actions of a person's everyday life, as in *Lady Sealing a Letter,* and the exceptional visual qualities of unexceptional still-life objects. More than a century later, Chardin's style was an important influence on Cézanne, who applied Chardin's interest in still life as an appreciation of form, rather than strictly an exercise. It wasn't until after his death that Chardin was recognized for shifting the still-life emphasis from technical display to formal organization.

About the Artwork

Chardin eliminated overt detail from his paintings in order to concentrate on natural forms. Many of his compositions were relatively abstract, and he used muted tones, subdued colors and detailed textures.

About the Media

Chardin painted in oils with thick, layered brushstrokes and thin, lustrous glazes. Later in life, as his eyesight began to fail, Chardin began creating pastel works, many of which are now very valuable.

About the Technique

The realistic quality of Chardin's work was achieved through a slow, thoughtful process. Before applying paint to his canvas, Chardin would set up a still life and make sketches of it in pencil and charcoal. His oils were applied carefully, although he was more concerned with capturing the play of light and composition in his paintings than with showing accurate detail.

Artist Profile

John Singleton Copley
1738–1815

John Singleton Copley (jän sing´ gəl tən kä´ plē) was born in Boston one year after his parents arrived from Ireland. His father died, and his mother supported the family by running a tobacco shop. When Copley was 11, his mother married Peter Pelham, who was a printmaker, a painter, and a teacher. Pelham quickly saw young Copley's talent and gave him his first art lessons. Copley also learned from studying prints of paintings by Michelangelo, Raphael, and Rubens. In 1774, he was encouraged to go to Europe to study. He left his family in Boston and toured Europe. His father-in-law was one of the importers of the famous shipment of tea that was dumped in Boston Harbor. Because of that incident, his father-in-law left the Colonies in anger, taking Copley's wife and children with him to London. Copley also went to London, where he enjoyed brief success.

About Art History

Copley was one of the finest American artists of colonial times. In his early paintings, Copley wanted to show people as they were. His paintings were said to be "more real than real." After he moved to England, his work was influenced by British and other European painters. It lost some of its energy and realism.

About the Artwork

Among Copley's early portraits were those of such American patriots as Paul Revere and John Hancock. He also painted English patriots who opposed America's independence. After moving to England, Copley began painting dramatic historical events.

About the Media

Copley worked primarily in oils.

About the Technique

Copley brought life to his early paintings by including objects used by his subjects in their daily lives. He was especially skillful at depicting his subjects' eyes. Through their eyes, he tried to show their characters. At first his art was appreciated and earned high prices. But he was not used to painting a portrait in one five hour session, as was the custom in London, and he soon fell out of fashion. His life ended on a sad note; he was in debt and lonely for his life in America.

Artist Profile

Salvador Dalí
1904–1989

Salvador Dalí (sal´ və dôr dä lē´) was born in Spain and grew up in a prosperous family. During his childhood he spent summers in a small coastal village in Spain, where his parents built his first studio, and many of his paintings portray his love of that area. Dalí earned fame and recognition early in his career with exhibitions in both Europe and the United States, and he continued to receive attention throughout his career, which spanned many styles and artistic experiments. Dalí was a surrealist, and he considered his paintings to be "dream photographs." He explored many different techniques and materials which influenced the surrealist movement everywhere. He moved to America and then Spain, where he opened the Teatro Museo.

About Art History

Surrealism was founded by the French writer André Breton, who was involved in the Paris Dada movement after World War I. He believed that art should free human behavior, so he published his *Manifesto of Surrealism* that expressed the necessity of humans to liberate their unconscious and communicate their personal desires. In 1928, Dalí joined this group of surrealists and took part in dream analysis, free association, automatic writing, word games, and hypnotic trances in order to discover the larger reality, or "surreality," beyond everyday ideas of rational logic. He swiftly became the leader of the surrealist movement, which included artists such as Joan Miró, André Masson, and Max Ernst.

About the Artwork

The Persistence of Memory is based on Dalí's childhood memory of a doctor asking to see his tongue. Melting watches drip over a tree limb and table, and a fleshy, alien creature draped at the painting's center is a grotesque image of Dalí's own profile with a limp tongue protruding from his nose. Ants, a representation of the passage of time, attack a pocket watch and symbolize decay in a dreamlike landscape. This painting is one of the most celebrated paintings of the twentieth century and combines reality and dreams, landscape and technology, and the symbolic and the irrational.

About the Media

Dalí worked in many media, including oil paints, watercolors, and pen and ink. He also created sculpture.

About the Technique

Sometimes Dalí relied on dreams to provide subject matter for his paintings, and he referenced the theories of Sigmund Freud in his painted explorations of personal fears and fantasies.

▲ **Leonardo da Vinci.** (Italian). *Self-Portrait.* c. 1512
Red chalk. 13 1/8 × 8 3/8 inches (33.3 × 21.3 cm.). Royal Library, Turin, Italy.

Artist Profile

Leonardo da Vinci
1452–1519

Leonardo (lē ə när´ dō də vin´ chē) was born in 1452, in the small Tuscan town of Vinci. He was the son of a wealthy Florentine notary and a peasant woman. Even when he was a child, people noticed that he had remarkable abilities. He had gracious manners, a fine sense of humor, great strength, and a curiosity that drove him to explore everything. In the mid-1460s, the family settled in Florence, Italy, where Leonardo was given the best available education. He was apprenticed to Verrocchio as a studio boy in 1466. By 1478, he was recognized as an independent master painter.

About Art History

Leonardo's work is considered the high point of Renaissance art. Leonardo was a genius whose achievements spread into many fields. The young Leonardo wrote, "It is easy to become a universal man," and so he did. He was an engineer, architect, inventor, physician, musician, and astronomer. His designs for the helicopter, tank, and other inventions have been constructed and powered by modern engineers. He wrote everything in mirror writing, a way of writing backwards that can be read by viewing the reflection in a mirror.

About the Artwork

One of Leonardo's most famous works is the *Mona Lisa,* which he carried with him on trips. Another is *The Last Supper,* which took him three years to complete.

About the Media

Leonardo painted in oils, tempera, and a mixture of the two. Some of his experimental paint combinations caused his artwork to flake away. He also worked in sculpture, and designed costumes and play sets.

About the Technique

Leonardo used shadows to make his subjects look three-dimensional. He blurred backgrounds and created aerial perspective.

Artist Profile

André Derain
1880–1954

André Derain (än drā´ də ran´) was a French artist who studied engineering before deciding to become a painter. After attending art school in Paris, he served three years in the military, painting in his free time. Derain's friend Matisse encouraged him to exhibit his paintings. Soon Derain was considered part of Matisse's *fauves,* a group of painters who used brilliant, almost violent, colors in their artworks. Derain also began to sculpt, first in wood and then in stone. He liked to try different artistic styles and did not hesitate to return to traditional approaches. During Derain's lifetime, some people rejected his work when it no longer seemed to be on the cutting edge of modern art. His work is greatly admired today.

About Art History

Derain's artistic style was influenced by Gauguin, Cézanne, Matisse, Picasso, and his extensive readings in philosophy. He studied many painting styles, from primitive to Renaissance, and he experimented with different techniques. His painting *The Barges* is fauvist, and his *Collioure,* a seaside scene, is impressionistic. *The Window,* a view of a cross on a hill, is realistic. Derain did not admire originality; instead, he tried to use the best of the past in his work.

About the Artwork

Derain painted still lifes, portraits, and landscapes. He also painted scenes with religious references, such as *Calvary,* in which dishes and a coffeepot on a table represent the Last Supper. Derain was fascinated with ballet and theatre. He designed costumes and sets for several productions. He also created paintings and woodcuts for book illustrations.

About the Media

This artist expressed his ideas in oil paintings; wood, stone, and steel sculptures; drawings, lithographs, woodcuts, and etchings; and clay masks and figures.

About the Technique

Derain studied art styles extensively and made numerous sketches and drawings before choosing a way to portray a specific subject. His approach to art was thoughtful and analytical rather than emotional.

Artist Profile

Gustave Eiffel
1832–1923

French architect Gustave Eiffel (g$\overline{oo}$s´ täv ī´ fəl) was born in Dijon, France, to a prosperous family. His mother was the reason for their prosperity, because she had started a coal business to ensure that Gustave received a good upbringing and education. She was a strong, intelligent woman and passed her work ethic down to her son. After graduating from college, Eiffel worked for a metal construction company, where he learned many architectural techniques. He began his building career at the early age of 26 when he was given his first independent assignment to build a bridge. Among his more famous creations are the Eiffel Tower and the framework for the Statue of Liberty. At the end of his life Gustave Eiffel moved toward scientific philanthropy.

About Art History

Seven years after the completion of the Bordeaux Bridge in 1860, Eiffel founded his company, Levallois-Perret. He and his crew were renowned for their construction of large metal structures, as well as bridges that could be dismantled or removed, attractive attributes for both business and military purposes. Gustave Eiffel's ingenuity led to the efficient construction of the Eiffel Tower, completed in 1889.

About the Artwork

The Eiffel Tower was built by Eiffel in collaboration with Maurice Koechlin and Emile Nouguier on Paris's Champs-de-Mars from 1887 to 1889. Built in only 26 months, Eiffel created it for the 1889 World's Fair as a symbol of France's industrial power and leadership in the field of civil engineering. In its first year after completion, the Tower received two million visitors. It continues to be one of history's great landmarks and hosts visitors from around the world year round.

About the Media

The Eiffel Tower is composed of 18,038 metal parts and weighs a total of 10,100 tons, a proportionally light weight for its height of 324 meters. With 1,665 steps, it attracts millions of visitors who come to climb and ride elevators to its peak in order to look out over the city of Paris.

About the Technique

Before construction could begin, Eiffel made endless drafts, calculations, proposals and plans for the Tower. He prepared the construction site by gathering all of the tools and machinery construction would require, including self-propelled cranes. Each piece of the Tower was drafted to within one tenth of a millimeter, and arrived at Eiffel's factory in 12,000 parts ready to be assembled on site. A team of 250 workers completed the Tower's speedy construction.

Artist Profile

Randy Ellett
b. 1959

Randy Ellett (rân´ dē el´ let) was born in Gainesville, Georgia, and grew up in a family that encouraged him to make art. His father was a dentist who used the intricately detailed work of his profession to create cast jewelry. Ellett's mother continues to paint and draw today. Having artistic parents meant that art materials were always accessible in his childhood home. Ellett also took drawing classes when he was young, and had one of his drawings published right after graduating from high school. This early success further encouraged Ellett's artistic path as he went on to receive a degree in printmaking from the University of Georgia and establish a career in printmaking and woodworking.

About Art History

Ellett admires the work of Rembrandt von Rijn, Albrecht Dürer, and M. C. Escher, three of the leading printmakers in history. Dürer, a German Renaissance artist during the late 1400s, specialized in engraving and was known for his prints of religious iconography. The Dutch artist Rembrandt was renowned for his painting and printmaking and was the first to popularize etching as a major form of artistic expression in the 1600s.

About the Artwork

Ellett's piece *National Parts* was directly influenced by his experience working as a forklift driver in a warehouse. While working with a forklift he moved objects around the warehouse on wooden pallets. The writing and images on the pallets inspired *National Parts,* which is a large, hanging rectangle made from pieces of wooden pallets. Each piece has some writing on it, and many pieces display the name of a town, state, or country.

About the Media

In addition to woodworking Ellett works with printmaking. He primarily works with etching, a printmaking technique originally used to decorate armor and other metal products.

About the Technique

In the etching process a metal plate is coated on both sides with an acid-resistant varnish that dries a hard surface. The artist then draws a sharp needle to form through the coat of varnish and exposes the metal plate. This is easier than cutting directly into the metal. When Ellett achieves his desired composition, he covers the plate with acid which eats into the metal exposed by the drawn lines. By regulating the length of time that different parts of the plate are in acid he can make shallow, thin lines or deep, wide lines. The varnish is then removed from the plate before ink is applied and an impression is made on paper. If a change needs to be made Ellett can scratch away lines with a sharp metal scraper.

Artist Profile

James Ensor
1860–1949

James Ensor (jāmz en´sor) was born in Ostend, Belgium. Except for three years when he studied at the Brussels Academy, he li was born in Ostend, Belgium. Except for three years when he studied at the Brussels Academy, he lived in Ostend his entire life. A member of a group of progressive artists called *Les Vingt (The Twenty)*, Ensor was considered to be a master by the time he was only 20 years old. He was interested in masks and portraying the nature of people in Belgium in a sometimes carnivalesque manner. As he grew older the negative criticism he received for his art caused him to become cynical and reclusive.

▲ **James Ensor.** (Belgian).
Self-Portrait with Hat.

Pinacotea Nazionale di Ferrara, Italy.

About Art History

Ensor's earlier works were traditional still lifes, portraits, landscapes, and interiors painted in rich colors and subdued light. That changed when he was introduced to impressionism in the 1880s, and the earlier grotesque imagery of the Flemish painters Hieronymus Bosch and Pieter Bruegel the Elder. His harsh, violent themes and colors had a meaningful influence on twentieth century painting, as well as surrealism and expressionism. Although he continued to paint these avant-garde colorist scenes until his death, Ensor's style remained much the same after 1929.

About the Artwork

Ensor was fascinated with masks and often portrayed them. Even his representations of people on holiday in Belgium were mask-like. He was disgusted with their natures, and would portray them as clowns or skeletons in violent, garish colors. In Ensor's opinion these people were stupid, and so he painted them smirking, vain, and frightening. His landscapes were also created in a violent manner, as seen in the eruptive color and brushwork of his painting *Fireworks*.

About the Media

The intense colors of Ensor's work were created with oil paints. The pigment in this paint is quite rich and concentrated, and he usually painted on larger canvases that further heightened the impact of his subject matter.

About the Technique

The eerily mask-like features of Ensor's subjects, as well as the vigorous application of paint in his landscapes, were made by using quick brushstrokes and a palette knife.

Artist Profile

Minnie Evans
1890–1987

Minnie Evans (min´ ē ev´ ənz) was born in North Carolina. She left the state only once in her life. She went to school through the sixth grade, and had no training in art. Yet she said, "Something told me to draw or die." She started drawing in 1925 and continued for the rest of her life. Evans first used crayons and later created collages. All of her work expressed her vision of the relationship between God, people, and nature. She worked as a maid and a gatekeeper at Airlie Gardens in Wilmington, North Carolina. Her art hangs in the permanent collections of museums as far away as Switzerland.

About Art History

Evans used the colors of Caribbean folk art and the complex designs seen in Byzantine mosaics. Her work might be considered surreal, as her drawings came from her visions, not from seeing other artwork or studying art styles.

About the Artwork

Evans often drew a human face in a garden paradise. She wanted to show that God is in nature through the blaze of colors. The time Evans spent at Airlie Gardens inspired her to paint the brilliant flowers and lush plants that fill her work. One of her best-known collages, *Design Made at Airlie Gardens,* overflows with faces and plants.

About the Media

Evans worked in oils, watercolors, pencil, pen and ink, crayon, and collage.

About the Technique

Evans said she never planned a drawing or painting; it just happened for her. She simply transferred the vision in her mind to paper. Sometimes she reused earlier drawings by pasting them onto cardboard or canvas and then combined them with new designs in oils and watercolors.

Artist Profile

Paul Gauguin
1848–1903

As one of France's leading postimpressionist painters, the artistic career of Paul Gauguin (pôl gō gan´) did not begin until he was a 25-year-old stockbroker. He decided to become a painter when he saw the first impressionist exhibit in Paris, France, in 1874, and throughout the next 30 years he developed his own style independent from impressionism and full of influences and experiences from his life. He was not content or fulfilled in Europe, however, and in 1891 he left his family and job to move to Tahiti and various other destinations in the South Pacific. With the exception of a two-year absence, Gauguin remained in Tahiti for the rest of his life, painting until his death in 1903.

About Art History

Through his encounters and friendship with van Gogh, Pissarro, and Cézanne, Gauguin developed a passion for expression through color. In the 1880s, he painted in France and created landscapes similar to those of Pissarro.

About the Artwork

Gauguin's style is a conceptual method of representation. His subjects, mainly women, are painted in flat, bold colors emphasizing a wild, almost untamed environment. His exposure to primitive art in Tahiti can clearly be seen in the rich colors in pieces such as *Faaturuma*. A woman's surroundings are painted in bright, earthy tones and her dress is a warm rose color that brings her image even closer to the viewer. Gauguin's ties with impressionism were, at this point, behind him. He had finally found his own style in a new land.

About the Media

Gauguin's portraits were created in oils on canvas. When he painted in France, he also used pastels for some of his landscapes.

About the Technique

The colorful, flat appearance of Gauguin's paintings was achieved by using large brushes and brushstrokes. Many of his paintings were created by sketching and studying models, and the expressive nature of his surfaces reflects the influence of the primitive art of the South Pacific.

Artist Profile

Alberto Giacometti
1901–1966

Alberto Giacometti (äl ber´ tō jä kə me´ tē) was born in an Italian-speaking area of Switzerland. He had an artistic background as his father, Giovanni, was a famous post-impressionist painter. As a child he loved to make art and was most interested in illustrating stories, and he had great confidence in his early drawing ability. His confidence was challenged, however, when his father pointed out that Alberto continued to depict objects in small dimensions no matter how hard he tried to capture them in a larger size. This diminishment of size reappeared in his later career with figurative sculptures that grew smaller and smaller. He was finally able to create taller figures, but they retained a sticklike thinness that now characterizes his work.

About Art History

In his youth Giacometti was inspired by the murals and frescoes of Tintoretto and Giotto and the paintings of Alexander Archipenko and Paul Cézanne. He went to study in Paris in 1922, and had his first one-man exhibition in 1927, which earned him sudden success and put him in touch with the Parisian avant-garde. Two years later he joined the surrealist group, but gradually moved away from their style toward an increasing amount of work with the human figure. In the 1940s, his tendency towards existentialism was mirrored by his growing friendships with Simone de Beauvoir, Pablo Picasso, and the philosopher Jean-Paul Sartre, whose theories declared that humans were alone in a meaningless universe but able to choose our own fate. Giacometti became internationally known for his sculptures and paintings, and was the recipient of respected sculpture prizes later in his career.

About the Artwork

Thin, fragile bronze figures walk aimlessly across a bronze slab in Giacometti's *City Square*. Their sketched appearances make them look like stretched human forms rather than proportional bodies. The artist became well-known for his elongated figures and concentrated on three basic themes: the walking man, the seated portrait, and the standing female nude. In addition to their slender, tall and roughly textured dimensions, Giacometti's figures often had very small heads and huge feet that rooted them to the ground.

About the Media

Giacometti created numerous portraits in oil on canvas that can be identified by their delicate, weblike lines.

About the Technique

When Giacometti shifted again toward figurative work during the war years, he worked from live models and then from memory, creating a number of heads and busts and later full figures out of bronze. The heavy nature of bronze in *City Square* seems to contradict the waifish proportions of Giacometti's figures.

Artist Profile

Grandma Moses
1860–1961

Anna Mary Robertson Moses (an´ a mâr´ ē ro´ bərt sən mō´ zəz) was always interested in art but was too busy raising children and doing farm work to devote much time to her creative talents. It was not until she was in her late 70s that she took up painting. In 1938 her work was discovered when an art collector saw one of her paintings hanging in a drugstore window. Within two years her work was being exhibited at the Museum of Modern Art and the Galerie St. Etienne, both in New York City. In the last 20 years of her life, her paintings appeared in museums and galleries throughout the United States and Europe. She continued to paint until the year she died at age 101.

About Art History

Grandma Moses is regarded as a *folk,* or *naïve,* painter because she never had any formal training. She had to invent her own techniques to depict her subject matter. Even though some critics did not take her seriously, her paintings were popular and were reproduced on posters, fabrics, plates, and greeting cards.

About the Artwork

Landscapes were among Moses's favorite and most frequently painted subjects. Her paintings do not follow the conventions of perspective but rather rely on scale and color to create an illusion of depth.

About the Media

Moses preferred board to canvas because it made a painting more durable. Pressed wood is a type of fiberboard often used for insulation or paneling. She applied paint in thin, opaque colors. It is likely that Moses chose to work with oils because of their versatile color range, durability, and the fact that the color does not change as it dries.

About the Technique

Moses began her paintings by treating a board with one coat of linseed oil. She then applied three coats of flat white house paint to the board to create a neutral ground. Over this she sketched rough details with a pencil. From her lifelong work with embroidery and textiles, Moses learned how to break things down into separate sections of color. The effects of this method caused some critics to compare her work to an impressionistic style.

Artist Profile

George W. Hart
b. 1955

Even in elementary school, George Hart (jôrj hart) was building. He created a giant sculpture out of thousands of toothpicks. He went on to receive a bachelor's degree in mathematics from MIT, a master's degree in linguistics from Indiana University, and doctorate degrees in electrical engineering and computer science from MIT. He has taught at Columbia and Hofstra universities.

About Art History

Hart is the author of more than 60 scholarly articles, conference papers, and technical reports. He has lectured, shown his artwork, and given workshops across the country and in Europe, including at the New York Academy of Sciences and at Harvard University. In 1999 he received an Individual Artist Award from the New York State Council for the Arts and a grant to create *Book Ball,* a geometric construction of books celebrating the millennium.

About the Artwork

Hart's constructive sculptures range in size from very small to eight feet in diameter. A 16-foot mobile hangs in the student center of Hofstra University. All the pieces are mathematically engineered. His work deals with patterns and relationships derived from classical ideals of balance and symmetry. The colors in each piece are found naturally in the media, such as silver or plastic silverware. He sometimes works with various colors of wood for contrast or paints metal with bright colors for the spherical pieces.

About the Media

Hart uses a variety of media, including paper, wood, plastic, metal, and compilations of common household objects such as silverware, pencils, compact discs, or toothbrushes.

About the Technique

Hart mentally visualizes a piece for days or years and then may spend up to a month making jigs for constructing the object. He also makes many sketches or paper models to see how a finished product will turn out. Hart spends a lot of time testing various glues, solders, and paints to prevent any drips, splashes, or detection of joints in his work.

Artist Profile

Marsden Hartley
1877–1943

Marsden Hartley (märz´ dən härt´ lē) was born Edmund Hartley in 1877 in Lewiston, Maine. His mother died when he was eight, and when he was 16 he went to live with his father and stepmother in Cleveland, Ohio. It was there that he began his formal art training. After winning an art scholarship, Hartley attended New York's National Academy of Design. In New York he became friends with Alfred Stieglitz who ran 291, a vanguard art gallery in the early 1900s where Hartley had his first solo exhibition. As he progressed as an artist his style constantly changed, yet he continued to address the importance of an individual's connection with nature.

▲ **Richard Tweedy.** (American). *Marsden Hartley.* 1898.

Oil on canvas. 26 × 18 inches (66.04 × 45.72 cm.).
National Portrait Gallery, Smithsonian Institution, Washington, D.C.

About Art History

Hartley painted with contemporaries such as Arthur Dove, John Marin, and Georgia O'Keeffe, and he was influenced by impressionism. His earlier paintings reflect the styles of Cézanne, Matisse, and Rodin, and echo the writing of Thoreau, Emerson, and Whitman. Hartley was inspired by these writers and their transcendentalist ideas, which placed importance on a person's ability to experience a direct connection with nature. Hartley traveled widely throughout his career.

About the Artwork

As Hartley's environment changed rapidly in the early 1900s, so did his style. He often used vigorous brushwork to emulate the impressionists. This energetic expression can be seen in his paintings of the mountains in Maine. Whether in America or Europe, Hartley exhibited a rawness, and he used broad, deliberate forms in paint that sometimes seemed to slash the canvas. Hartley created a military series in Berlin from 1913 to 1915, using rhythm and repetition, along with bold colors, military insignia, and numbers to express the vibrant culture he experienced there. From 1917 to 1918, Hartley painted in a regionalist style. In 1918, his visit to New Mexico inspired him to paint landscapes and still lifes that were analytical and two-dimensional. By the 1930s, Hartley had returned to painting landscapes.

About the Media

The majority of Hartley's paintings were done in oil paints on canvas. Later in his career he created a large number of pastel drawings.

About the Technique

Hartley's bold paintings were created using quick, broad brushstrokes and heavy paint. Sometimes he would fracture the plane of his paintings in a cubist style, and at other times he would use repeating patterns such as a checkerboard to emphasize swift, energetic movement.

Artist Profile

Ferdinand Hodler
1853–1918

Ferdinand Hodler (fer´ də nənd hō´ dlər) was born the son of a carpenter in Bern, Switzerland. When he was 14 he was apprenticed to a landscape painter, and at age 18 he studied with another landscape artist in Geneva. He received practical, thorough training but was much more interested in depicting real feelings than simply learning technique. He traveled throughout Europe, broadening his style and experiencing the many artistic movements of the late 1800s that prompted him to paint portraits in addition to his landscapes. Later in his career Hodler focused on painting colorful mountain scenes.

▲ **Ferdinand Hodler.** (Swiss). *James Virbert, Sculptor.* 1907.

Oil on canvas. $25\frac{3}{4} \times 26\frac{1}{8}$ inches (65.41 × 66.35 cm.). The Art Institute of Chicago, Chicago, Illinois.

About Art History

Hodler was fascinated by legend, history, the primitive, and the tragic, and looked beyond his formal training to find inspiration. In 1878, he traveled to Spain where he encountered currents of impressionism. A trip to Paris in 1881 exposed him to the work of Neo-impressionists George Seurat and Paul Gauguin, whom he greatly admired. Hodler became a symbolist painter, and his work is similar to that of the symbolist Pierre Puvis de Chavannes, although Hodler used brighter colors and more stylized forms. He exhibited in the 1889 Paris World Exhibition and the 1890 Paris Salon to a mix of criticism and acclaim. Hodler was awarded a gold medal in Munich in 1897. In 1904, a large exhibition was held in Hodler's honor at the Vienna Sezession.

About the Artwork

As a *symbolist* Hodler used a rhythmic repetition of line and shape in his compositions and emphasized his subjects' decorative and mystical elements. In his piece *James Vibert, Sculptor,* the artist's visible brushstrokes serve as patterns among the brightly colored palette and massive shapes of his subject's portrait. Repetition of line is seen in the stylized beard and folds of the shirt.

About the Media

The majority of Hodler's works were painted in oils on canvas.

About the Technique

By using light washes in the backgrounds of his paintings, Hodler was able to draw the viewer's attention to his use of repetitive brushstrokes and varied patterns. Sometimes his stylization was apparent, as in his portrait of James Vibert, and at other times it was more subdued, as in *Portrait of the Artist in a Rage.*

▲ **Katsushika Hokusai.** (Japanese). *Hokusai as Warrior.* c. 1830.

Artist Profile

Katsushika Hokusai
1760–1849

Katsushika Hokusai (kät sōō´ shē kä hō´ kōō sī) was born in the city that is now Tokyo. He changed his name more than 30 times. No one knows why. When his home became dirty, he moved. He lived in 93 different places! Hokusai supported himself by illustrating comic books, greeting cards, and novels. During his lifetime he had two wives and seven children.

Hokusai was not interested in money. To pay his bills he would hand over an envelope of money he had received for a painting. Sometimes it was enough, and sometimes it wasn't. When he was broke, he bought art supplies after dark, hoping to avoid people he owed. Hokusai painted constantly during his later years, barely eating enough to stay alive. He averaged one painting a day, and created 30,000 pieces of art in all.

About Art History

Much of Hokusai's artwork was in a style called *ukiyo-e,* or "floating world." This style focused on nature and people doing everyday things. Hokusai introduced Eastern art to the West. His work strongly influenced other artists such as Manet and Degas.

About the Artwork

Hokusai is best known for his many paintings of Mount Fuji. In some the volcano is framed by an ocean wave. In others, it appears in the background as people go about their daily tasks. Hokusai also painted common Japanese subjects, such as dragons, pagodas, actors, and acrobats.

About the Media

Hokusai was famous for his colored prints on woodblocks. He used a separate block of wood to print each color. He also created oil paintings, ink drawings, and watercolors.

About the Technique

Hokusai was a master of brush painting. He used a brush with a tip that was round and pointed instead of flat. Brush painting can show both hard outlines and soft strokes. As Hokusai grew older, his brushstrokes became softer and less controlled. He began to use transparent washes of colors rather than opaque paint.

Artist Profile

Frida Kahlo
1907–1954

Frida Kahlo (frē´ dä kä´ lō) was born in Mexico. Her life was short and painful. As a child she had polio, which caused one leg to stop growing. At 18, she was severely injured in a bus accident. Thirty-two operations did not ease her pain entirely and it often kept her in bed. Whenever possible she dressed in richly embroidered outfits, wore much jewelry, and tucked flowers in her hair. At 22, she married the famous painter Diego Rivera. He was 42 at the time and had been married twice before. Kahlo and Rivera lived in separate houses connected by a bridge. Despite their stormy relationship, she wanted to have children and was deeply disappointed that they could not. After winning wide recognition for her painting, the frail Kahlo died at age 47.

About Art History

Kahlo is often grouped with the surrealists, but she was more interested in personal expression than dreams and fantasies. She used symbols to represent her feelings. For example, a skeleton, representing death, often appeared in her work. She also created an imaginary friend, her twin. She showed the twins sitting together in the painting *The Two Fridas*. An artery joins their exposed hearts.

About the Artwork

Kahlo used her life as the subject for much of her work. She painted her own birth, her bus accident, her marriage to Rivera, and scenes depicting her physical pain. Kahlo said she painted portraits of herself because she was often alone.

About the Media

Kahlo worked in oils on small canvases, often about the size of a sheet of paper.

About the Technique

Kahlo painted precisely, carefully controlling her brushstrokes. In her later work she used specific colors to express emotional states. Yellow expressed madness, sickness, and fear. Cobalt blue represented love.

Artist Profile

Louisa Keyser (Dat So La Lee)
1850–1925

Louisa Keyser (lü ē´ sə kī´ zər) was a Washoe Indian born in Nevada. Her handwoven baskets were quite valuable during her lifetime and are now exhibited in museums and collections throughout the country. Keyser's baskets are even more impressive because she was nearly blind. The extreme precision with which she created her artwork is especially inspiring; she could barely see her own artwork and yet it was perfectly made. With her innovative new styles and techniques Keyser changed the nature of traditional Washoe basket making.

About Art History

Keyser was a member of the southern Washoe, and her native people from the Great Basin have been making baskets for thousands of years. While Keyser was alive her tribe experienced many changes and was dwindling in number and losing their land. In order to earn a living she went to work as a maid for Amy and Abraham Cohn, who were owners of a successful men's clothing store. Amy Cohn was very interested in Native American culture, and she and her husband bought many baskets from Washoe weavers. They then sold the baskets to art collectors for large sums of money. In 1895, the Cohns grew so impressed with Keyser's basketry that they offered her full financial patronage in exchange for ownership of all her baskets. For 25 years Keyser and her husband were supported by commissions from the Cohns.

About the Artwork

The designs and patterns on Keyser's basketry ranged from simple patterning to cultural narrative. By 1897, Keyser was credited with creating the spheroid style of basketry called *degikup*, which most Washoe weavers copied. A *Degikup* was a large basket that curved in at the top and was covered with surface designs. The red designs were made from redbud dye and the black designs were made from bracken fern.

About the Media

Washoe baskets were made from natural materials native to the area. Fern and dried grasses were often woven into the baskets and were stitched with thin strands of natural string or fibers.

About the Technique

Each strip of grass or fiber of Keyser's basket can be seen in her geometric and evenly spaced designs. Keyser began her baskets with a tightly stitched coil of bracken fern and then wound coil after coil from right to left out from the center. The baskets achieved their decoration and patterning from dyed bracken that formed stacked v-shaped designs. Each year she gathered natural materials and cured, seasoned, and stored them in anticipation for the next season.

UNIT 6 • Lesson 5

Artist Profile

Gustav Klimt
1862–1918

Born in Vienna, Austria, Gustav Klimt (goos´ täv klimt) grew to become one of the leading forces behind his country's art nouveau movement. When he was just 14, Klimt became a student at the School of Applied Arts in Vienna, where he and his brothers studied a variety of techniques. He was highly regarded for his early murals, decorative art, and flowered landscapes, but his primary interest was painting sensuous portraits that celebrated the female figure. He was not interested in the crowded bustle of society but preferred the solitude of his studio and flower garden.

About Art History

Along with his brother Ernst, and Franz Matsch, Klimt began his artistic career creating commissioned murals and ceiling paintings for the Burgtheater and the Kunsthistorisches Museum in Vienna from 1886 to 1892. He later focused on portraiture and was fascinated by decoration and the figural emphasis of painter Hans Makart. This influence stayed with Klimt throughout his career, especially when he incorporated the style of *horror vacui* into his work, filling every minute area of canvas with detail. In 1898, Klimt was a cofounder and the first president of the *Vienna Sezession*, a group of modern artists and architects whose independent exhibitions and style initiated the Viennese version of Art Nouveau. He was a mentor to the younger painter Egon Schiele, and together the two men were regarded as Vienna's leading Sezession artists.

About the Artwork

The Vienna Sezession style often incorporated the aesthetic and psychological aspects of Vienna's intellectual culture of the early 1900s. Klimt's work revolved around themes of regeneration, love, and death. The majority of his portraits celebrated the sensuality of women, as in his famous paintings *Danae* and *Water Serpents II*. The stylized and decorative nature of art nouveau can be found in his paintings, and sometimes his patterns and details become subjects in themselves.

About the Media

Klimt used oil paints and often built square canvases for his compositions.

About the Technique

Klimt always had female models in his studio, whether he was painting portraits of them or not. His skill as a draftsman was renowned, and more than 3,000 of his drawings and studies remain. Many of these drawings depict the sensuous models of his studio and wealthy female patrons of the Viennese social elite. As he aged, Klimt's refined brushwork turned toward a more loose, expressive nature, though he continued to create compositions from a combination of live models, photographs, and drawings.

Artist Profile

Susan LeVan
b. 1947

Computer artist Susan LeVan (sōō´ zən luh´ vân) was born and raised in Michigan. She received a bachelor of arts degree in anthropology from the University of Michigan and a master of fine arts degree in printmaking from the Cranbrook Academy of Art. Her background in printmaking filters into her current work with digital imaging. It also influenced her earlier work with mixed media. In 1991 LeVan shifted from an emphasis in mixed-media collage to a focus on computer graphics using this technique. She continues to create her vividly colored computer paintings today.

About Art History

Many artists have influenced LeVan, including Pablo Picasso, Henri Matisse, and Native American and folk artists. Picasso was one of the predominant forces in the abstract and cubist movements and has become well known for his highly gestural abstract paintings and collages. Matisse, the leading fauvist painter in the early 1900s, promoted wild color and abstraction. The primary colors and expressive compositions of Matisse's work are echoed in LeVan's creations, which have been included in a number of international illustration annuals including *Communication Arts*, *Print*, *How*, and *The Society of Illustrators*.

About the Artwork

LeVan's artwork uses bright, bold colors to create stylized images and compositions. Patterns and abstract forms characterize her work, and she often uses pronounced outlines to define her shapes. It is typical for LeVan's figures to have unnatural color schemes, as with her image *Kid,* in which she depicted a child with one lime green eye, one yellow eye, and a face made from sections of blue, red, and gray.

About the Media

LeVan uses a computer with a pressure-sensitive graphics tablet. She works with software that allows her to imitate natural media such as watercolor, chalk, and pencil, and also allows her to create compositions that appear to be handmade.

About the Technique

LeVan's computer software lets her create imagery in much the same way a painter would use paints and brushes. She begins with a sketch of an image on the computer, prints it, creates a collage, and then scans the finished piece.

Artist Profile

Christina Lemon
b. 1967

Christina Lemon (kris tē´ nə le´ mən) is an artist, educator, and scholar. She received an undergraduate and a master of fine arts degree in jewelry design and metalsmithing. Currently she is a professor of art, teaching all levels of metalsmithing at Georgia Southern University. Her metal jewelry is well known for its textured designs and polished surfaces.

About Art History

Lemon's work is inspired by her interest in African masks and ethnic jewelry. African masks are often recognized by their stylized, geometric shapes and decorative or symbolic patterning. Lemon integrates these qualities into her own one-of-a-kind jewelry and blends her knowledge of ethnic art into her designs. She exhibits frequently and continues to create work that expresses a unique and evolving style.

About the Artwork

Texture is important in Lemon's work, and a variety of techniques are used to enrich the metal surfaces of her jewelry. In *Mask Series Brooch,* she brought together various shapes and layers of material to create texture. Straight lines, curved and zigzag edges, smooth metal, squiggle cutouts, and a raised hemisphere come together in this piece to create a unified symphony of form. A *brooch* is traditionally worn as a pin on a person's clothing.

About the Media

Lemon's *Mask Series Brooch* is made from sterling sheet and 18 karat bimetal, a unique metal made from bonding sterling silver and gold to create a two-color material. Sterling silver is an *alloy,* or mixture, of 92.5 percent silver and 7.5 percent copper.

About the Technique

Lemon forms her metal over wooden stakes with the use of plastic mallets. She uses *solder,* a metal alloy, to permanently join the metals. To be effective, the solder must melt more easily than the metals to which it is applied. There are two kinds of solders, hard and soft. *Hard solder* is very strong and can be pressed or hammered into different shapes without breaking. Some hard solders can be drawn out into long threads, and others can be made into metal sheets. *Soft solders* are weak and cannot be hammered without breaking.

Artist Profile

Stanton Macdonald-Wright
1890–1973

Stanton Macdonald-Wright (stan´ tən mək dä´ nəld rīt) was born in Charlottesville, Virginia. He ran away from home at the age of 11 to Los Angeles, California. He studied at the Art Students League and later attended art school in Paris, France, where he developed a painting style called synchromism. Upon returning to the United States, Macdonald-Wright settled in New York and California to focus on his new avant-garde methods, which spanned a career of more than six decades. Later in life he studied Eastern philosophy and painted in an Asian-influenced style. He lived in California and Kyoto, Japan.

About Art History

Macdonald-Wright began his modernist painting career in conventional art academies and studied in Paris from 1907 to 1912. However, he felt the traditional Sorbonne art classes stifled his creativity, and he became inspired by the radical approaches of cubism, fauvism, futurism, and orphism. He was influenced by the work of Matisse, Rodin, and Percyval Tudor-Hart. He met Morgan Russell in France, and the two artists began the synchromism movement, which emphasized color and expression. Following shows in Paris and Germany, Macdonald-Wright and Russell brought this new style with them when they returned to America in 1914, and they exhibited across the country. During the 1930s, Macdonald-Wright was the seven-states regional director of the Works Progress Administration art program. He taught iconography at UCLA from 1942 to 1952.

About the Artwork

Synchromism was based on the idea that color and sound are equivalent phenomena, and that a painter can arrange colors the way a composer can arrange musical notes. With this in mind, Macdonald-Wright and Russell employed a system of color scales that allowed color to compose form and depth in a composition. In *Conception Synchromy,* this energetic use of color indicates shape and depth, even though it uses no identifiable forms. This system was one of the first abstract, nonobjective styles in American art.

About the Media

Macdonald-Wright painted in oils on canvas, arranging his compositions with attention to a balance of color and movement. He also created the first full-length, stop-motion film in color. Macdonald-Wright created 500 pastel drawings and designed synchromatic theater sets for this film.

About the Technique

Macdonald-Wright's brushstrokes are as energetic as his color scale, often giving his paintings a sense of rapid or flowing movement. He layered paints over one another in some areas, which made the forms appear as if they were floating into one another and redefining their shapes on the canvas.

Artist Profile

Franz Marc
1880–1916

Franz Marc was born in Munich, Germany, in 1880. He began his formal studies of art at the Munich Art Academy, but studied on his own as well, traveling to Paris, France to see the works of Van Gogh, Gauguin, and the impressionists. In 1911, he and the artist Wassily Kandinsky began a network of German and Russian abstract painters called *Der Blaue Reiter,* or The Blue Rider, group. Marc was fascinated by the idea of mood and symbolism in color, as well as the natural forms of animals. Many of his works show horses or cows in various bright, saturated colors. Marc joined the military and served in World War I. In 1916, at the age of 36, he was killed in battle in France.

About Art History

Franz Marc is considered to be one of the key contributors to the birth of modern abstract art. He and other members of The Blue Rider group experimented with color, form, and lines in ways the art world had never seen before. This earned them a reputation for being daring, bold, dramatic, and shocking. They were more diverse than the fauves or Die Brücke and intended to influence their viewers through the sheer power of color. Marc explained that his work came not from the real world, but from the visions of his inner mind. Themes of natural beauty, spirituality, and the expression of emotions through color can be seen in much of Marc's work.

About the Artwork

Marc began his career as a naturalist and evolved into expressionism before meeting Kandinsky, with whom he agreed that blue was the spiritual color of maleness. Bright colors dance across his canvases, sometimes in curving arcs as in his painting *The Large Blue Horses,* and sometimes in woven, overlapping fronds as in his 1914 painting *Animals in a Landscape.* In Marc's work the intense color is frequently the main subject. The brilliant colors are observed before the subject is discerned, which achieves Marc's goal of communicating through color.

About the Media

The majority of Marc's paintings were oils on canvas. He also created many woodcuts and charcoal drawings.

About the Technique

The bright, expressive lines and forms in Marc's work were created with wide brushes and bold fields of color. He did not always blend his pigments to show gradation or depth. Instead he used gestural brushstrokes and defined outlines to make contrasting shapes that vibrated with deep color.

Artist Profile

Henri Matisse
1869–1954

Henri Matisse (än´ rē ma tēs´) was the son of a middle-class couple in the north of France. He was not interested in art while he was in school. After high school his father sent him to law school in Paris. When he was 21 an appendicitis attack changed his life. Because he had to spend a long time in the hospital, his mother brought him a paint box to help him pass the time. Matisse eventually convinced his father to let him drop out of law school and study art. Matisse married and started a family soon after. His paintings were not selling, so he worked for a decorator and his wife opened a hat shop. During the last years of his life he suffered from arthritis. Unable to hold a brush in his hands, he devoted his efforts to making paper cutouts from papers painted to his specifications, and he created fantastic, brightly colored shapes. Unlike many other artists, he was internationally famous during his lifetime.

About Art History

In 1905, Matisse and his friends exhibited a painting style that showed strong emotionalism, wild colors, and distortion of shape. They were called *les fauves,* or "the wild beasts," and they experimented with intense, sometimes violent colors. Without letting their work become abstract, Matisse and other fauvist painters tested the bounds of reality.

About the Artwork

Matisse painted still lifes, room interiors, and landscapes. His paintings of dancers and human figures were generally more concerned with expressive shapes than an accurate representation of anatomy.

About the Media

Matisse painted primarily with oils, and also created many prints. Later in life he worked with cut paper.

About the Technique

Matisse worked with bold, intense colors. He simplified and distorted shapes for expressive qualities. He was most interested in the way visual elements were organized.

Artist Profile

Edvard Munch
1863–1944

▲ **Edvard Munch.** (Norwegian). *Self-Portrait.* 1881–1882.
Oil on canvas.

Edvard Munch (ed´ värd mungk) was born in Norway in 1863. He and his family moved often, and he was frequently ill, which caused him to miss school and eventually receive his education through private lessons. He received his first drawing lesson as a young boy and continued learning drafting skills in technical school as a young man. Munch did not have a very happy life. When he was five years old, his mother died from tuberculosis, and in 1875 he almost died from the same disease. Three years later his favorite sister died just as their mother had. These tragedies filtered into his work, and death became one of his most constant themes. As an artist Munch initially faced a difficult world. The general public rejected his frank treatment of death, and progressive artists and critics were negatively shocked by his work.

About Art History

After studying in Norway, Munch spent several years in France and Germany, where he was influenced by the Nabis and post-impressionists. Along with van Gogh, Munch is regarded as the main influence on German expressionism. His painting *The Scream* has come to symbolize the mental angst of civilized man. In 1908 Munch suffered a nervous breakdown and returned the following year to Norway, where he spent the rest of his life.

About the Artwork

Munch was inspired to paint *The Scream* by an evening walk he had taken through the city. He had walked on a path alongside a fjord, feeling ill and tired, and all at once he sensed a "shriek passing through nature." Munch translated this experience into the painting through the figure's skull-like head blood-red clouds, and a swirling, linear environment that expresses anxiety. The painting seethes with movement, as though the figure's scream is actually shaking his surroundings and vibrating the surface on which he is painted.

About the Media

Most of Munch's paintings involved dark or glaring colors jarring against one another in harsh lines and expressions of despair. After his nervous breakdown his palette became brighter and his motifs changed. He began to look for more optimistic and universal symbols. He painted in oils and tempera and created many charcoal drawings, often in fast, expressive strokes.

About the Technique

Munch often painted outdoors, and referenced live models for his paintings and sketches.

Artist Profile

Juan Muñoz
1953–2001

Born in Madrid, Spain, Juan Muñoz (hwän moon´ yōs) was convinced he did not want to grow up to become an artist, but when he ran away from home to London at the age of 17, he worked and studied printmaking, easing himself into a career as an artist. He traveled often in the 1970s, searching for his own style and producing little work. In the 1980s, he began to create famous installations and bronze figures and participate in major exhibitions throughout Europe.

About Art History

Muñoz created his installations with contemporaries, such as Robert Gober, Charles Ray, Kiki Smith, and Stephan Balkenhol. His work has been compared with the writings of Jorge Luis Borges, the music of Alfred Schnittke, and the architecture of Francesco Borromini.

About the Artwork

The bronze figures in *Last Conversation Piece* can best be compared to the appearance of punching-bag dummies. Despite their massive weight, these mysterious figures seem to be rocking on their rounded bases, resembling toys made of cloth and beanbag. Instead they are almost life-size casts of bronze, gesturing to one another and acting out an obscure narrative. Muñoz was inspired by ventriloquist dummies when he first began this project, as well as the dwarves painted by Diego Velázquez and the dancers painted by Edgar Degas. Their postures express urgency and concern, and the figures outside the immediate circle of conversation appear to be rushing to enter the dialogue, but are forever unable to move.

About the Media

Juan Muñoz's sculptures and installations involve a wide variety of materials ranging from bronze to resin to the actual street or warehouse where his art is installed. He considered an installation site to be just as important as the sculpture itself, and paid great attention to the role of the spectator.

About the Technique

Muñoz's bronze figures were created through a process of casting. The artist would construct his sculptures from pliable materials, make a mold of the finished product, and then pour bronze into the mold, filling in the cavity formed by the first sculpture. Bronze captures the texture and dimension of flexible surfaces while creating a permanent form, such as Muñoz's conversing statues in *Last Conversation Piece.*

Artist Profile

Alice Neel
1900–1984

Alice Neel (a´ləs nēl) was raised in rural Pennsylvania but abandoned her working middle-class heritage to pursue art and political activism. She began painting when it was difficult for a woman to receive critical recognition, especially if the woman ignored the prevalent style of American abstraction, which is what Neel did. Without the aid of a studio or sales, Neel developed her own style and painted numerous compositions of her friends, family, fellow artists, neighbors and famous contemporary figures. By the time she was in her 60s, Neel finally began to receive national attention, which continued throughout the rest of her career.

About Art History

Neel's early life was full of challenges. Though she graduated from the Philadelphia School of Design for Women in 1925, her education and individuality were overlooked by galleries and museums. She was often desperate—she was frequently impoverished, her daughter died in childhood, she suffered a nervous breakdown when her husband left her, and she was hospitalized for a year following an attempted suicide. She also lost more than 100 paintings when a boyfriend destroyed her work in a fit of rage. Through it all Neel continued to paint and incorporated her leftist ideology into her art. She was elected to the American Academy and Institute of Arts and Letters in 1976.

About the Artwork

Neel's early work tended to depict generalized relationships, but as her work evolved she began to portray the particular personalities of unique individuals. Neel often exaggerated the physical features of her subjects, especially their eyes, because this was a way to further express their nature. This emphasis on figures did not make her a portraitist, however. In *Loneliness,* Neel completely omitted the presence of human form to depict a scene of solitude. Muted colors emphasize the emptiness of a lone chair sitting before a window looking out on another window. Though one would expect to find traces of humanity in the view, there is no human in sight.

About the Media

Neel painted most often with oils on canvas.

About the Technique

Neel relied on observation and memory to create her paintings.

Artist Profile

Louise Nevelson
1900–1988

Louise Nevelson (loo ez´ ne´ vəl sən), one of the most important and successful American sculptors of the twentieth century, was born in Kiev, Russia. Her family resettled in Rockland, Maine, when she was five years old. As a child she began assembling wood scraps from her father's contracting business. Her education was rich and varied, including music, theatre, dance, and visual art. She studied in New York, New York and Paris, France. At first she made both paintings and sculptures, but eventually concentrated on sculpture, which she exhibited irregularly from the 1930s onward. It was not until the late 1950s that she began to receive critical acclaim. Before her death, she had received more public commissions than any other living sculptor.

About Art History

During the twentieth century the art of Africa, Oceania, and pre-Columbian America was studied. Artists also began to take interest in the visual and mythic powers these cultural artifacts possessed. Louise Nevelson was influenced by tribal and Mayan art. Her work has a modern, totemic power that links contemporary art styles to ancient civilizations.

About the Artwork

By painting her sculptures all black, white, or gold, Nevelson transformed the typical meanings of her found elements. These elements are combined to express both formal and thematic concerns. Toward the end of her career she worked with more abstract, geometric shapes. Many of her large public sculptures are made from steel.

About the Media

Nevelson used found wooden objects to create many of her works.

About the Technique

The paint on Nevelson's sculptures unifies the many shapes, but allows the grain of the wood to show through, giving liveliness to the abstract forms.

Artist Profile

Georgia O'Keeffe
1887–1986

Georgia O'Keeffe (jôr´ jə ō kēf´) was born in Sun Prairie, Wisconsin. At the age of ten she began taking private art lessons, but the thing she liked most was experimenting with art at home. By 13, she had decided to become an artist. She trained under experts and won many prizes for her art. For years she challenged the art world with her unique vision. She eventually became famous for her spectacular, larger-than-life paintings of natural objects, including flowers, animal skulls, and shells. She loved nature, especially the desert of New Mexico, where she spent the last half of her life. O'Keeffe was married to the famous American photographer Alfred Stieglitz and appears in many of his photographs. In 1997, a Georgia O'Keeffe Museum opened in Santa Fe, New Mexico. It is the first museum in the United States devoted exclusively to the work of a major female artist.

About Art History

Stieglitz promoted modern artists and photographers from Europe and America through a magazine called *Camera Work* and a gallery known as "291." O'Keeffe and the circle of artists she met through Stieglitz were pioneers of modernism in the United States. She took subjects into her imagination and altered and simplified their appearances. She expressed her emotions through her vivid paintings.

About the Artwork

O'Keeffe's artwork features bold, colorful, abstract patterns and shapes. She most often painted natural forms such as flowers and bleached bones, pulling them out of their usual environments. She never painted portraits but sometimes painted landscapes.

About the Media

O'Keeffe used oils and watercolors for her paintings. She used pastels, charcoal, and pencil for her drawings.

About the Technique

O'Keeffe worked in dazzling, jewel-toned colors. She chose unusual perspectives, such as very close up or far away. She also enlarged the scale of her subjects.

Artist Profile

Nam June Paik
b. 1932

Nam June Paik (näm jōōn pāk) is considered a pioneer of video art. As a child growing up in Korea, Paik was fascinated by electronics, especially the radio. When television was introduced in the early 1950s, he became interested in technology and cultural iconography. With the encouragement of his friends, Karlheinz Stockhausen and John Cage, Paik became involved in electronic art and combined ideas of composition and performance. Regarded as a father of video art, he continues to influence and teach younger generations of artists and to provide cutting-edge technology for the art world.

About Art History

When the Korean War began, Paik and his family fled to Tokyo, Japan, where he studied philosophy, aesthetics, art history, and music. After graduating in 1956 from the University of Tokyo, he went to Germany and received training as a pianist, musicologist, and composer. At that time Germany was the center of the electronic music scene, and Paik began to fuse his love of art, electronics, and music into video art installations. He became involved with the neo-Dada art movement Fluxus and returned to Japan to conduct experiments with electromagnets and color television. This combination of technology and innovation provided Paik with a way of making moving paintings with sound.

About the Artwork

Inspired by the changing nature of society, Paik uses video to express the complexities of contemporary culture. In *Eagle Eye* he assembled nine computer keyboards and televisions into the shape of a bird's wings and tail feathers. Blue neon light shines behind the bird to indicate the atmosphere of a Native American thunderbird. The video screens contain pulsating imagery of satellite photographs of Earth and a solar eclipse, as well as images of missiles being launched. The juxtaposition of these two events hints at both the foresight and blindness of humanity.

About the Media

Paik considers video to be similar to a painter's canvas. Many of Paik's video pieces consist of numerous television screens with multiple videos playing simultaneously. This collaborative and overwhelming effect of the many screens bombards the viewer with information and invites consideration about society's relationship with television.

About the Technique

Through the use of computer programming and digital editing, Paik captures video footage and then projects, displays, and arranges it in sequences on one or many video screens.

Artist Profile

Giovanni Pannini
1691–1765

Giovanni Pannini (jō vän´ nē pä nē´ nē) was born in 1691 in Piacenza, Italy. As a child Panini planned to pursue a religious career, but his education in perspective and architectural painting navigated him toward a life in architecture and painting. He first trained in illusionistic painting under a stage designer in Piacenza and then moved to Rome to study figure drawing. Though he created portraits, decorative frescoes and stage designs, he specialized in decorations and *vedute,* or view, paintings. Panini also designed buildings, carvings, festival decorations, and furnishing for churches.

▲ **Giovanni Pannini.** (Italian). *The Picture Gallery of Cardinal Silvio Valenti Gonzaga.* 1749.

Oil on canvas. $78\frac{3}{16} \times 105\frac{3}{8}$ inches (198.6 × 267.67 cm.). Wadsworth Atheneum, Hartford, Connecticut.

About Art History

Early influences on Pannini's work included the paintings of ruins by Giovanni Ghisolfi, the landscapes of Jan van Bloemen and Andrea Locatelli, and the topographical views of Gaspar van Wittel. By 1716, he was making real and imaginary views of Rome's ancient and modern monuments, and he established himself primarily as a fresco decorator of the palaces of Roman aristocracy. He taught at the Accademia di San Luca during the 1720s and 1730s, and in 1732 he received the rare honor of becoming a member of the Academie Royale de Peinture et de Sculpture in Paris, France. In the 1740s and 1750s, Pannini painted numerous views of ancient and contemporary Rome to meet the demands of foreign visitors.

About the Artwork

Pannini's paintings are clear, bold, elegant, and perfectly drafted. His precise drawing skills influenced his contemporaries and many younger artists, and his paintings of festivals, ceremonies, and dignitaries' visits captured contemporary events in history. In *The Picture Gallery of Cardinal Silvio Valenti Gonzaga,* Pannini portrayed the cardinal's elaborate and large art collection. The viewer is drawn to the central figure dressed in red who admires the art around him. Monumental arches and the long hall in the painting also engage the viewer. Not only did Pannini exhibit excellent draftsmanship in his perspective and details, but he also painted a replica of each work of art in Gonzaga's gallery.

About the Media

Pannini's view paintings mark the pinnacle of his career. The two main types of view paintings were *vedute prese da i luoghi,* carefully and accurately rendered views of actual places, and *vedute ideate,* imaginary views and combinations of buildings and monuments.

About the Technique

Pannini worked from numerous sketches and studies of his subjects. He also set up his studio in different locations in order to capture specific lighting, detail, perspective, and color.

Artist Profile

Pablo Picasso
1881–1973

Pablo Picasso (pä´ blō pi kä´ sō) was born in Málaga, Spain. He did poorly in school but his father, an art teacher, taught him to draw and paint. Picasso learned quickly. When he was only 14 he had a painting accepted for an exhibition. Picasso moved to Paris, France when he was 18. At the time he was very poor. Thieves stole what little he had, yet they left his now valuable drawings. In time the outgoing Picasso made many friends. Among them were the American writers Ernest Hemingway and Gertrude Stein and the Russian composer Igor Stravinsky. Picasso painted at night and slept late most mornings. He worked hard his entire life. He completed 200 paintings the year he turned 90.

About Art History

Picasso was one of the most influential artists of the 1900s. He experimented with many styles and created new ones. He invented the style known as cubism. He took 18 months to paint his first cubist picture, *Les Demoiselles d'Avignon,* which shows five women from several angles. Other artists were soon copying his style.

About the Artwork

Picasso's paintings changed as his life changed. When he was poor, he painted sad pictures in shades of blue. This style is called his *Blue Period.* When he fell in love with a neighbor, he painted happier pictures in shades of pink. This style is called his *Rose Period.* Then came his cubist period, and later he painted in a style that reminded viewers of Greek sculpture.

About the Media

Picasso created drawings, oil paintings, ceramic pieces, sculptures, prints, and engravings. He also invented collage along with the French artist Georges Braque. They combined colored papers, newspaper, old illustrations, and small objects with painting and drawing to produce collages.

About the Technique

In his cubist paintings, Picasso simplified his subjects into circles, triangles, and other basic shapes. He often outlined these shapes in black or a bright color.

UNIT 1 • Lesson 6
UNIT 3 • Lesson 4
UNIT 5 • Lesson 6

Artist Profile

Harriet Powers
1837–1911

▲ **Harriet Powers.** (American). *Pictoral Quilt.*
c. 1895–98.

Cotton with cotton and metallic yarns.
$68\frac{7}{8}$ × 105 inches (174.96 × 266.7 cm.).
Museum of Fine Arts, Boston, Massachusetts.

Harriet Powers (ha´ rē ət pou´ ərz) was born in Athens, Georgia. She and her husband bought a small farm where they raised 11 children. Powers earned money by raising chickens, working as a seamstress, and making patchwork quilts until she died in 1911. Although she did not gain fame as a quilt artist in her lifetime (everything she owned at her death was worth a total of $70), her exquisite quilts now are appreciated by visitors to the Smithsonian Institution, and the Museum of Fine Arts in Boston, Massachusetts.

About Art History

Story quilts were an alternative way to communicate for people who could not write well. It is regrettable that we know so little about Powers. Luckily Jennie Smith, who bought Powers's first quilt, kept a record of some of her interactions with its creator. Many quilts made during this time bear no credit to the artists that created them. Quilting bees were common during this period, with four women working on each quilt. The first team to finish would win the bee. No men were allowed to attend the event, but after the sewing was finished the men joined the women for a quilting party. Powers met her future husband at one of these events.

About the Artwork

Although quilting is an ancient art form, an African-influenced artistry shows through in the quilts made by Powers. Usually the needlework on quilts was done in geometric shapes and flowers, but Powers added unique forms, such as animals, sunbursts, and stars. Powers is known to have sewn at least two quilts between 1886 and 1898. Stitched in bright colors, her appliqué on the first quilt tells biblical stories. Her second quilt incorporated tales of events recent to her.

About the Media

Powers used fabric scraps and thread to complete her quilts. Some decorative metallic thread was used to highlight the detail of the quilt.

About the Technique

Appliqué quilts contain cloth stitched to a background fabric. These quilts spotlight a needleworker's skills, as the designs are incorporated into the fabric. The patterns in the fabric create feelings of motion, while the dark and light colors set the mood for each story depicted.

Artist Profile

Rosalind Ragans
b. 1933

Rosalind Ragans (ro´ zə lind rā´ gənz) was born and grew up in New York City. When she was 11, polio paralyzed the right side of her body. Fortunately two years of therapy helped her regain nearly all the movement she had lost. Ragans had planned to be a stage designer but discovered that she loved teaching art. She began teaching in New Jersey in 1956. She earned a doctoral degree in education. While teaching art in Georgia in 1975, she began developing *ArtTalk*. This art education program presents art as a language, or way of communicating. Published in 1987, it has been well received by art teachers across the nation. Since then Ragans has created *Art Connections,* which you are using now. She still finds time to create the batik paintings she loves.

About Art History

Ragans works in a style of her own that approaches abstraction. Like two artists she admires, Alice Neel and Frida Kahlo, she uses her art to deal with personal conflicts. For example. Her *Self Portrait,* subtitled "My Soul Dances," expresses her mind's ability to dance even though her body cannot.

About the Artwork

All of Ragans's batik paintings have dancers and plants in them—either as the main subject or hidden in the background. Ragans has always loved music and dancing. She is also fascinated by plants because she saw so few of them as a child in New York City.

About the Media

Ragans uses dyes and untreated rayon, cotton, linen, and silk to create her batiks.

About the Technique

After sketching an image on fabric, Ragans uses hot wax to cover the areas she wants to remain white. Then, she applies the colors, beginning with the palest ones. After each color dries, she covers it with hot wax so that it will not be affected by later colors. The last step is removing most of the wax with paper towels and an iron. Any remaining wax adds a glow to the image.

Artist Profile

Pierre-Auguste Renoir
1841–1919

Pierre-Auguste Renoir (pyâr ō goost´ ren wär´) was one of the most widely known and best-loved European painters. The sixth of seven children, Renoir was born into a poor family in Limoges, France. His father was a tailor, and the family had to live in a slum, with few luxuries or comforts. Renoir showed signs of talent at an early age in many artistic fields. Although he was a talented singer, he became an apprentice at a porcelain factory, where for five years he copied French masterpieces onto plates and soup tureens. During this apprenticeship Renoir developed his brushwork and his passion for the eighteenth century French master painters such as Watteau and Boucher. Renoir's work became more widely known in the 1880s, after a decade of struggle and lack of recognition.

About Art History

Renoir was one of a group of artists known as the impressionists. These artists, including Monet, Pissaro, Sisley, and Morisot, followed the advice of the poet Baudelaire to abandon historical subjects and to show the beauty of modern life instead. In attempts to record truthful and direct responses to nature they painted outside rather than inside the studio. They painted quickly in order to capture the scenes in front of their eyes before they changed. The impressionists were known for their bold, rapid technique. They covered the surfaces of their canvases with broken touches or slashes of color. The impressionists began exhibiting in 1874, and were met with extreme criticism and public hostility. Many people were unable to understand their style. Today, exhibitions of impressionist artists are greeted with much excitement.

About the Artwork

Renoir studied art for two years at the famous École des Beaux-Arts in Paris, France. He learned to draw there, but he disregarded academic guidelines that did not allow him to develop his own personal style. He discovered a new style of painting not based on the feathery brush strokes of impressionism. During this period, he also began to concentrate on using women and children as his subject matter.

About the Media

Renoir most frequently used oils or pastels.

About the Technique

Renoir painted on a white background. For the first layer of color he used paint so diluted that it ran down the canvas. Then he would cover the surface of the canvas with tiny brushstrokes of pure color.

Artist Profile

Timothy Rose
b. 1941

Timothy Rose (tiˊ mə thē rōz) was born in Washington, D.C., and is widely known for his whimsical mobiles and painted murals. His artistic mobiles begin as watercolor or mixed media drawings that explode with color and energy, then translate to a three-dimensional creation through a series of balancing experiments. He has lived in Japan, Mexico, and France, and currently lives in California. His studio is located on Mare Island, near San Francisco.

About Art History

When Rose began exhibiting in 1965, his creations had a definite linear quality to them, reminiscent of the simplistic, almost comical nature of Alexander Calder's work. After he graduated in 1968 with a degree in anthropology from San Francisco State University, Rose traveled to Paris and was introduced to the work of Wassily Kandinsky. He was inspired by Kandinsky's drawings of overlapping layers of floating shapes and began to incorporate them into his later creations.

About the Artwork

Rose's mobiles employ a great sense of lightness, both in physical presence and character. The lighthearted aspect of his brightly colored hanging sculptures creates a feeling of swift movement, and the different dangling shapes add to their whimsical and explosive appearance. In the eight-foot-long mobile *Double Pan Swoosh* the artist uses suspended circular disks and elongated s-curve pieces of stainless steel to capture an undulating "swoosh" motion in the air. With each individual piece bobbing slightly on its wire, the overall composition of the mobile sways in and out as though it were alive.

About the Media

Each mobile is made of stainless steel or burnished steel pieces attached to stainless steel wires.

About the Technique

Rose begins each of his mobiles from the bottom up. First he lays out the shapes he wants to use on a big sheet of paper and draws lines connecting the bottom or end pieces. This gives him an idea as to how the shapes will hang. He connects the small end pieces with wire first and then progresses to connect the middle-size systems. Once the pieces are connected, he adds the top bar, balancing the systems of shapes from the bar before fastening the final wires.

Artist Profile

Susan Rothenberg
b. 1945

Susan Rothenberg (soo´ zən rô thən berg) was born in Buffalo, New York. She attended Cornell University and took classes at the Corcoran School of Art and George Washington University in Washington, D.C. When she moved to New York City in 1969, she studied dance and eased her way into the abstract expressionist art scene of the 1970s. This background in dance and performance contributed to her appreciation of movement, and she became fascinated with depicting speed and movement on canvas in her abstract horse paintings and later figurative works.

▲ **Susan Rothenberg.** (American). *Cabin Fever.* 1976.
Acrylic and tempera on canvas. 67 × 84 $\frac{1}{8}$ inches (170.18 × 213.67 cm.). Modern Art Museum of Fort Worth, Texas.

About Art History

Rothenberg admired the abstract expressionist artists Philip Guston, Jackson Pollock, Willem de Kooning, and Clyfford Still, and their influence can be seen in her work. Rothenberg's big entry into the art world came from her employment as an assistant to the artist Nancy Graves in 1970. By 1973, she began showing her horse paintings, and this led her to work with the human figure in the 1980s. Critics regarded this evolution as a rebirth of the figure in modern painting. In 1990, Rothenberg moved from New York City to the Southwest, and her art took on the images and character of her Santa Fe environment.

About the Artwork

The horse paintings for which Susan Rothenberg is known originally began as horse silhouettes, simple outlined images on large canvases. They were painted with great expression and usually involved only one color. This gave the paintings a sense of immediacy. She often divided her compositions with a vertical line running down the center of the canvas. In *Cabin Fever* she uses the swift application of paint and a large canvas to emphasize the silhouetted horse's speed. The animal exists in a minimalist form because only its essential shape is shown.

About the Media

In the 1970s and 1980s, Rothenberg used tempera and acrylic paints in her horse and figure compositions. By the mid-1980s, she became interested in expressing a sense of motion and speed in images of jugglers, dancers, and bicyclists. She began to use more oil paints in these images and in the images of her Southwest ranch.

About the Technique

For paintings such as *Cabin Fever,* Rothenberg would draw a gestural outline of the horse directly onto the canvas with charcoal or paint and then use wide brushes to apply paint thickly. Her work balances abstract form with recognizable subject matter, and this balance draws similarities between her earlier silhouetted paintings and prehistoric drawings found on cave walls.

Artist Profile

Henri Rousseau
1844–1910

Henri Rousseau (än rē´ rōō sō´) was born in a small town in France. When he was young he played the clarinet. He also spent some time in the French army. At the age of 25 he moved to Paris, where he spent most of his life. For a long time he worked as a customs clerk. He never went to art school. He learned to paint by practicing in gardens around the city.

◀ **Henri Rousseau.** (French). *Myself* (detail). 1890.

Oil on canvas. $57\frac{1}{2} \times 44\frac{1}{2}$ inches (146 × 113 cm.). National Gallery, Prague, Czech Republic.

About Art History

Because Rosseau had no formal art training, he is classified as a self-taught artist. The elements of fantasy and mystery in many of his paintings influenced the art movement of surrealism in the 1920s.

About the Artwork

Most of Rousseau's paintings look unlike anyone else's. In his first paintings he portrayed people and places around Paris. His most famous paintings are exotic portrayals of deserts and jungles. Many include wild animals, such as lions and monkeys. Rousseau often painted pictures of people from faraway countries. His paintings are known for their details. In some he painted every leaf on every tree and every whisker on every animal. Many of his paintings evoke the same feelings as strange dreams.

About the Media

Rousseau generally worked in oils on canvas. He mixed his colors well to make them look smooth.

About the Technique

Many people wondered where Rousseau got the ideas for his paintings. He told them that he had visited Mexico, but that was not true. He actually painted his jungle pictures by looking at the plants in the Paris botanical gardens. The animals were inspired by pictures he saw in books. He used dolls as models for people. Rousseau painted shapes very carefully to make his subjects look real.

Artist Profile

Julia Russell
b. 1949

Julia Russell (jōōl´ yə rə´ səl) grew up on a cotton farm in the delta of Mississippi. The people who worked the land sang sad songs and told stories in the evening about train hopping and panthers. Russell found that art was a way to keep these memories alive and educating others provided her an opportunity to share her memories. She began teaching art in the early 1970s in Memphis, Tennessee, and found that all children responded to respect and basic kindness. In 1997, she was named Tennessee art educator of the year. She was also awarded the Order of the Pearl by the Kappa Delta sorority for outstanding service to humanity. Russell began receiving recognition for her artwork in the early 1980s, winning numerous awards and receiving signature artist status from several professional organizations.

About Art History

As a young teacher who went through college in the late 1960s, Russell was ready to put free expression behind her and to rely on the masters of the Renaissance for instructional content. During this time she began to understand the art concepts behind the processes relating to her own work. Color, light, illusion of form, and perspective understandings are still evident in her curriculm designs and personal artwork. She started painting chairs in the late 1990s using acrylic paints, gold leaf, and a variety of glazing techniques. Chair art has become a new challenge—to bring a functional object into the realm of art.

About the Artwork

Russell's Leonardo da Vinci chair is one of a collection of tribute chairs honoring great artists of the past. This chair pays homage to one of the most popular artists of the high Renaissance. The combination of da Vinci's image and a flutter of butterflies throughout the design pays a silent tribute to the essence of one who lives on through the inspiration of others.

About the Technique

The linen fabric on the chair is first sealed with a coat of gesso, and then the image is painted with acrylic paints. When Russell uses gold leaf in certain areas she first paints those areas with a coat of black paint to add a crackled effect to the leafing. The chairs are finished with several layers of polymer gloss. *Polymer gloss* is a glaze formed by mixing small amounts of water with a clear polymer. To tone the gold leaf a teaspoon of umber color is added to the layers of glaze and applied only to the gold leaf.

Artist Profile

Moshe Safdie
b. 1938

Moshe Safdie (mō shā´ saf´ dē) was born in Haifa, Israel, and received his architecture degree from McGill University in Montreal, Canada, in 1961. He has been commissioned by cities around the world to create designs for public buildings and civic organizations. The Salt Lake City Public Library and the Peabody Essex Museum, both designed by Safdie, opened to positive acclaim in 2003. Safdie also designed the United States Institute of Peace Headquarters in Washington, D.C. and the National Campus for the Archaeology of Israel in Jerusalem.

About Art History

Safdie first began his architecture practice in Montreal after graduating in 1961. In 1970 he established a branch office in Jerusalem and became involved in the rebuilding of Jerusalem, joining together the old and new cities and creating a number of public buildings and museums. At this time, he also started working in Iran, Senegal, Singapore, and the northern Canadian Arctic. In 1978 Safdie relocated to Boston, Massachusetts, and became the Director of the Urban Design Program and a professor of architecture and urban design at Harvard. Many public buildings in Canada and the United States were designed by Safdie, and most of them have won international and national competitions.

About the Artwork

Safdie created *Habitat,* an innovative cluster of stacked modular apartments, for the 1967 World Exposition in Montreal. *Habitat* became one of the lasting twentieth-century icons of utopian urban living. These contemporary structures resemble the towns of Mesopotamia and the pueblos found in the southwestern United States, while promoting the interaction of the residential community. One side of *Habitat* faces the busy city streets of Montreal and the other faces a quieter river and trees. The people living in these apartments regard themselves as city-dwellers or forest-dwellers, depending on the environment outside their windows.

About the Media

In addition to *Habitat,* Safdie has created other housing developments and planned new communities, major cultural and civic projects, and a wide range of public and academic institutions.

About the Technique

Each apartment of Safdie's *Habitat* design is ready-made and stacked together in a variety of ways. Much like children's building bricks, these constructions are arranged on top of one another. Safdie's designs were expensive and difficult to build, but they introduced a new model of community living.

Artist Profile

Miriam Schapiro
b. 1923

Miriam Schapiro (mir´ ē əm shə pir´ ō) is an American artist who was born in Toronto, Canada. She grew up in the Flatbush section of Brooklyn, New York. Her parents encouraged her pursuit of a career in art and sent her to art classes at the Museum of Modern Art. She met her husband, artist Paul Brach, while attending college. They married in 1946 and have a son who is a writer. Schapiro organizes her home life so that art is woven into it. She can move from baking in the kitchen to painting in her studio and back to the kitchen without feeling interrupted. Her husband says that she has learned to live a "seamless life."

About Art History

In the beginning of Schapiro's career, her work was abstract expressionistic. Later she became an important leader in the feminist art movement of the early 1970s. She wanted art to speak as a woman speaks. In art history, women's art has been hidden. Even the materials that women have used—lace, fabric, tea towels, ribbon, sequins, buttons, rickrack, yarn, silk, cotton, and so on—have been left out of art history.

About the Artwork

In time, Schapiro's work became more geometric and structured. In the 1950s, she expressed her identity by including feminist themes in her art. In 1972, Schapiro and other female artists changed an old Hollywood mansion into a totally female environment and called it "womanhouse." Schapiro and Sherry Brody made *The Dollhouse*—a construction of bits of fabric and tiny household objects meant to reflect female life and fantasy. Schapiro also made "femmages." She and a few other artists invented this word to describe art made with techniques that women traditionally use, such as sewing, embroidery, piecework, and appliqué. *Femmages* are collages that reflect female emotions and creativity.

About the Media

Schapiro uses fabric scraps, sequins, buttons, threads, rickrack, spangles, yarn, silk, taffeta, cotton, burlap, wool, and other materials a person might use in daily life.

About the Technique

Schapiro uses collage, assemblage, and decoupage to join materials.

Artist Profile

Karl Schmidt-Rottluff
1884–1976

Karl Schmidt-Rottluff (kärl shmit rət lōōf) was born in Germany, and began his education as a student of architecture in Dresden. As a young man he abandoned his studies of architecture for painting and became an active self-taught German expressionist painter. With his passion for expressionism Schmidt-Rottluff became a co-founder of the avant-garde group of painters known as *Die Brücke (The Bridge)* in 1906.

◀ **Karl Schmidt-Rotluff.** (German). *Self-Portrait.* 1968.
Watercolor.

About Art History

The aim of the artists in Die Brücke was to seek a new, emotionally expressive style and move away from the traditional art forms of the early 1900s. Influenced by cubism, fauvism, and primitive art, these German expressionists included Ernst Ludwig Kirchner, Erich Heckel, and Emil Nolde. Schmidt-Rottluff was passionate about the group's deliberate detour from conventional technique.

About the Artwork

Schmidt-Rottluff's paintings are characterized by harsh, angular shapes and bold colors that clash on the canvas. Lithography, a form of printmaking, was also a passion of his, and his paintings often reflect the hard lines of his woodcutting. In his *Portrait of Emy* the mask-like, contorted face of the woman reflects Schmidt-Rottluff's interest in primitive art. The aggressive, unnatural colors vibrate against the rigid outlines of Emy's face, and her form is simplified to allow a greater emphasis on Schmidt-Rottluff's illusion of reality.

About the Media

By using forceful, glaring colors Schmidt-Rottluff expressed intense emotion in his paintings. Neutral tones played a small role in his compositions, although he eventually softened the overall harshness of his palette over the years. Oil paints allowed his colors to retain their vibrancy and depth, despite their flatness.

About the Technique

The abrupt outlines and angular quality of Schmidt-Rottluff's work were created by his use of concentrated blocks of color. He outlined the form of his subject and then added paint with gestural brushstrokes, often patching together areas of flat color instead of using a gradation of hue. He painted so expressively that sometimes he left sections of raw canvas visible and allowed the fabric's weave to show beneath the paint.

Artist Profile

George Segal
1924–2000

Not long before George Segal (jorj sē´ gəl) was born, his parents emigrated from eastern Europe to the Bronx in New York. They did not consider art to be a legitimate profession, but Segal insisted on studying art in college. After graduating in 1947, he started a chicken farm in New Jersey and taught at a high school to support his wife and two children. In 1958, he sold his chickens and used the buildings the chickens were housed in as his studio. For the next two years he created plaster figures on wood and chicken wire frames. All the art teachers in that area received surplus gauze embedded with plaster from a nearby Johnson & Johnson plant to give to Segal. He used this gauze to create his sculptures.

While teaching an art class in 1961, he hit upon the idea of making a plaster cast of his own body, removing the cast, and placing the hollow figure in a real-life setting.

About Art History
Segal's combination of painting and sculpture helped bridge the gap between abstract expressionism and pop art. He was influenced by Degas, Mondrian, Cézanne, and Picasso.

About the Artwork
Segal created scenes that focus on human relationships, such as the lonely figures in *The Gas Station* or *The Diner*. Segal drew attention to human events such as the civil rights movement and the Vietnam conflict. Some of his pieces have been controversial, such as *Kent State: Abraham and Isaac*. Although Kent State University asked Segal to create a monument to honor the demonstrators who were killed there, the university did not accept his finished work because it showed the violence about to be committed. This sculpture finally found a home at Princeton University in Princeton, New Jersey.

About the Media
At first, Segal used ordinary plaster to form his figures. In 1971, he switched to a more durable industrial plaster called *hydrostone*. Later he began casting sculptures in bronze.

About the Technique
Segal later formed his figures by wrapping a model in plaster-soaked bandages and removing them after they hardened. He placed his white plaster people into complex settings with real objects. He created a diner, a gas station, a street corner, and butcher shop, and then created an eerie effect by placing his stark-white plaster people with colorful real objects.

Artist Profile

William Sharp
1803–1875

William Sharp (wil´ yəm shärp) was born in London in 1803. He lived there until he was 36, and in 1839, he arrived in Boston, Massachusetts. While in London, Sharp worked as a lithographer and exhibited with the Royal Academy from 1819 to 1829. Shortly after his arrival in Boston, he gained recognition for his skill as a portraitist and color lithographer. In 1840, Sharp created the first color lithograph printed in the United States, and by the late 1840s, he was producing full-color lithography, or *chromolithography*. He died in Massachusetts in 1875.

▲ **William Sharp.** (English/American). *Great White Lily of America.* 1854.

Chromolithograph on woven white paper. $21\frac{1}{4} \times 27$ inches (53.98 × 68.58 cm.). Amon Carter Museum, Fort Worth, Texas.

About Art History

Lithography, a type of printmaking, was invented by Alois Senefelder in Germany in 1798, and appeared in England and the United States 20 years later. As soon as the technology arrived, artists attempted to create prints in color. After many challenges and improvements, lithography eventually became the chosen media for large-scale folio works and illuminated gift books. Chromolithography became less expensive when the steam-driven printing press was invented and inexpensive paper became available. By the 1880s, the process was used for magazines and advertising.

About the Artwork

In 1854, Sharp illustrated a book by author John Fisk Allen entitled *Victoria Regia: or, the Great Water Lily of America*. The Victoria Regia lily is a large tropical flower that was discovered by western scientists in 1801 in Central America. These illustrations were the earliest examples of large scale printing in the United States and documented the research of the lily's scientific properties.

About the Media

In addition to chromolithography Sharp was highly regarded for his landscape painting and was well-known for his illustrations of fruit and flowers.

About the Technique

Sharp drew or painted designs with greasy ink or crayons on specially prepared limestone. He then moistened the stone with water, which soaked into the areas not covered with crayon. An oily ink that adhered to the drawing, but not the water, was then rolled over the stone. A print was made by pressing paper to the inked drawing. A chromolithograph involves a different stone for each color, so a print is pressed each time a new color is used. Artists sometimes add detailed color or lines by hand after the print is made.

• Artist Profile •

David Smith
1906–1965

David Smith (dā´ vəd smith) was born in Decatur, Indiana. He studied art during high school through a correspondence course with the Cleveland Art School in Cleveland, Ohio. He then attended Ohio University in Athens, Ohio, and the University of Notre Dame in South Bend, Indiana. In 1926, Smith studied at the Art Students League in New York. He taught art at many colleges, including Sarah Lawrence College in New York, and Bennington College in Vermont. Smith became interested in the welded-steel sculptures of Picasso while studying in New York. Drawing on skills learned while employed in a car factory one summer, he used his welding experience to construct welded-steel sculptures. He was the first American to do so.

About Art History
Smith is considered an abstract expressionist. This style of art seeks pure expression through form and color. He was one of the most important American sculptors of the twentieth century.

About the Artwork
Smith often incorporated machine parts into his early sculptures. In the 1940s and 1950s he began to create delicate sculptures inspired by landscapes. Gradually his sculptures grew larger and simpler, and by the 1960s he was crafting huge, geometric works. Much of his work is two-dimensional and is intended for view from one side.

About the Media
Smith is best known for creating sculptures out of welded steel, but he also made ink prints and oil paintings.

About the Technique
Rather than casting metal sculptures in molds, Smith constructed his sculptures out of sheets of metal and wires. Smith polished some of his most famous outdoor sculptures so they reflected the sky, the sun, and the colors of nature.

Artist Profile

Wayne Thiebaud
b. 1920

Wayne Thiebaud (wān tē´ bō), one of California's most famous contemporary painters, has earned as many awards for excellence in teaching as he has for his painting and printmaking. He became interested in drawing in high school and later worked as a freelance cartoonist and illustrator. He continued his artwork during his military service in the U.S. Air Force during World War II. He drew cartoons for the military base newspaper. In 1949 Thiebaud decided to become a painter. His first one-person show in New York City was praised by the critics. At that time his subjects were mass-produced consumer goods, particularly junk food, and he was mistakenly classified with the pop artists. Later, he was classified as an American realist. His primary interest is organizing realistic subject matter into abstract compositions.

About Art History

Thiebaud arrived on the New York art scene in the 1960s when pop art was developing. He is sometimes identified as a pop artist because of the subject matter in much of his work. For example, many of his works show such objects as pinball machines, lipstick, and food. Thiebaud started as a realistic painter but later simplified his work, making it more abstract.

About the Artwork

Thiebaud reduces shapes to simple forms in his city landscapes. The viewer can easily identify circles, squares, triangles, rectangles, and arcs.

About the Media

Thiebaud paints with oils and acrylics, and creates a variety of prints.

About the Technique

Thiebaud tested mixing acrylic paint with oil paint, but he found that the mixture dissolved. He then tried painting oils over acrylics and discovered that he could achieve the effects he wanted. Before beginning to paint, Thiebaud stares at an object for a long time. Then he changes and adapts the object until it is the way he wants it in his painting.

Artist Profile

John Henry Twachtman
1853–1902

Born in Cincinnati, Ohio, John Henry Twachtman (jän hen´ rē twäkt´ mən) began studying art when he was 18. As his artistic style evolved, he moved from harsh, radical impressionist compositions to a calmer style. Near the end of his career, when he was painting some of his most famous works on his country farm, he came to believe that a person is most true and content in the solitude of nature.

About Art History

While studying at the McMicken School of Design in Cincinnati in 1871, Twachtman met his first mentor and professor, Frank Duveneck. The older artist invited Twachtman to share his studio and later to accompany him to Europe in 1875 where Twachtman studied at the Royal Academy of Fine Arts in Munich, Germany. He returned to the United States in 1878, and taught for a short time at the Women's Art Association of Cincinnati. From 1881 to 1885, the artist and his family lived in Europe. When he returned to the United States in 1886, he settled in New York and later bought a farm in Connecticut, where he painted some of his best-known landscapes. Twachtman was a founding member of The Ten, a group of American artists who joined together in 1897 to exhibit their work.

About the Artwork

Like impressionists, Twachtman strove to depict the impression of his subject rather than depicting the subject in detail. Impressionists also focused on dissolving the outlines of their imagery, and Twachtman did this as well, although he went a step further and made the outlines of his subjects melt into their environment. Twachtman was fascinated with the effect of the change of seasons on natural environments, and his country farmhouse supplied him with endless subject matter for this theme.

About the Media

Twachtman used a muted palette of oil paints.

About the Technique

The thick bands of color in Twachtman's compositions were painted in many layers, with the topmost layers allowing the bottom layers of color to emerge. Twachtman often applied paint with wide brushstrokes and showed only faint indications of form.

Artist Profile

Vincent van Gogh
1853–1890

▲ **Vincent van Gogh.** (Dutch).
Self-Portrait with a Straw Hat. 1885.
Oil on canvas. 16 × 12½ inches (40.6 × 31.8 cm.).
The Metropolitan Museum of Art, New York, New York.

Even as a boy in the Netherlands, Vincent van Gogh (vin´ sənt van gō´) cared about other people very much. He tried many jobs, including being a teacher, minister, and social worker. However, he had problems getting along with nearly everyone except his younger brother, Theo. At the age of 28, van Gogh decided that the best way he could serve others was through art. He expressed his deep feelings about people through his paintings. As he moved from place to place, he left many of his works behind. Some were burned in fireplaces for heat, and some were even used to patch holes in walls. Van Gogh was poor his entire life and often went hungry so that he could buy painting supplies. He died at age 37.

About Art History

Even though van Gogh sold only one painting in his lifetime, he is now considered the greatest nineteenth-century Dutch artist. He was one of the first to express his feelings through painting. This new school of art is now called *expressionism*.

About the Artwork

Van Gogh painted many different subjects, from portraits to landscapes. He once lived in France near fields of golden wheat and sunflowers, which he painted many times. He wrote that his sunflowers symbolized his gratitude toward others, especially his brother, who was one of the few people who encouraged him to paint.

About the Media

During the ten short years that van Gogh worked, he created hundreds of oil paintings, along with many drawings in ink, crayon, chalk, and charcoal.

About the Technique

Van Gogh wanted to show energy and motion in his work. He often put complementary colors, such as red and green, next to each other to add power to his paintings. He applied oil paints in thick layers, sometimes straight from the tubes. His thick layers, slashing brushstrokes, and swirling shapes give his paintings strong patterns that reflect his strong feelings.

▲ **Rembrandt van Rijn.** (Dutch). *Self-Portrait.* 1629.
Oil on panel. $35\frac{1}{3} \times 25$ inches (89.7 × 73.5 cm.).
Isabella Stewart Gardner Museum, Boston, Massachusetts.

Artist Profile

Rembrandt van Rijn
1606–1669

Rembrandt van Rijn (rem´ brandt vän rīn´) was the most influential Dutch artist of the seventeenth century. The seventh of nine children born to a miller and his wife, Rembrandt showed talent early in life. His parents took great interest in providing him with an education despite their modest income. Rembrandt studied a short time at the Leiden Latin School in the Netherlands to prepare for a profession as a city administrator. His parents eventually removed him from school and placed him in apprenticeships with painters. After moving to Amsterdam in 1631, he gained the commissions of several wealthy patrons and achieved great success. Rembrandt spent a large portion of the money he earned at auctions and his personal art collection. He encountered turbulent times both personally and financially, but he continued to produce works of art until his death in 1669.

About Art History

Most painters during the 1600s traveled to Italy to study art. Italian art and artists such as Michelangelo and Raphael were highly esteemed at this time. Rembrandt chose to remain in the Netherlands to learn about art. His remarkable ability to show feeling and emotion through dramatic lighting has made his work universally understandable and appreciated. Rembrandt is considered one of the greatest Western artists from all periods and countries.

About the Artwork

Under the painter Pieter Lastman, Rembrandt learned how to create dramatic accents using light and shadow, gesture, expression, and composition. In all, Rembrandt created more than 600 paintings as well as a large number of drawings, etchings, and more than 60 self-portraits. He most frequently created portraits, but he also completed paintings with historical, biblical, and mythological themes.

About the Media

Rembrandt worked mainly in oils on wood and canvas. He completed drawings on paper with pen and ink and also created etchings.

About the Technique

Rembrandt used a technique called *chiaroscuro*, an Italian word meaning "light and dark." He used light to focus attention on certain areas that contained details and left other parts in shadows using dark colors.

Artist Profile

John Warren
b. 1946

Born in Corona Del Mar, California, John Warren (jän wôr´ ən) grew up near the ocean where fishing, surfing, and diving were predominant sources of entertainment and occupation. He had a natural artistic ability that he began cultivating in high school, where he used painting and drawing to express his observations of the natural environment. The sea played an integral role in his compositions and continues to be a driving force in his studies and creations.

About Art History

Warren attended San Diego State University where he studied art and biology and majored in marine biology. He combined these two areas in a brief career as a scientific illustrator, and he used pen and ink to depict the biological organisms he studied. After he graduated, he moved to Hawaii, where the ocean again factored into his artistic pursuits, especially woodcarving. When he returned to California, Warren began working with architect Buckminster Fuller and gained a thorough understanding of geometry and the use of fiberglass. He also learned the techniques of welding and steel fabrication, which he used to create his later sculptures. His work reflects this array of skills, and he continues to work out of his studio in California.

About the Artwork

The influence of Warren's studies in marine biology can be found in his sculpted fish series, which showcases his knowledge of the creatures. *Dark Snapper* is made from welded pieces of sheet metal and is only one of many similar creations, all of which were modeled from the fish he studied.

About the Media

Welded sheet metal, rocks, and railroad ties come together in the creation of Warren's fish, which can be seen in *Dark Snapper*. The railroad ties form formidable teeth, and the planar silhouette of the fish contains a large rock in its center, giving its body and belly an organic core.

About the Technique

Warren cuts his shapes from large sheets of metal, carving designs and patterns into the form of the fish. He then welds the fins and body pieces together.

UNIT 1 • Lesson 4

Artist Profile

Max Weber
1881–1961

Max Weber (maks weˊbər) was born in a region of Russia that is now in Poland. In 1891, his family immigrated to New York City. Weber studied art at the Pratt Institute in Brooklyn, New York. He also studied in Paris and spent several months traveling through Europe. He returned to the United States to paint and write articles about art and color for *Camera Work,* a journal published by Alfred Stieglitz. In 1911, Stieglitz arranged an exhibition for Weber's work. Weber married in 1916, and taught art to support his wife and two children because his paintings were not selling. The art world was beginning to appreciate his work at the time of his 1930 exhibition at New York's Museum of Modern Art. Toward the end of his life he focused on sculpture. Throughout his art career Weber wrote poetry and essays about art.

About Art History

Weber, a leader of the modern art movement in the United States, was greatly influenced by Cézanne. Weber was friends with Rousseau and Matisse and admired the work of Picasso and Kandinsky.

About the Artwork

Weber's work includes portraits, landscapes, and still lifes. After World War I, Weber focused more on his Jewish heritage. He also experimented with nonobjective sculpture.

About the Media

In addition to oil paintings Weber created small sculptures, prints, watercolors, drawings, and woodcuts.

About the Technique

In his early cubist paintings Weber suggested figures using flattened spaces and blocks of bright color. In *Chinese Restaurant* he fragmented the motifs extracted from a Chinese restaurant, placing them in a distinctly cubist arrangement. In the 1930s, Weber used line more actively. In the 1950s, he reintroduced cubist distortion in his work.

Artist Profile

Akrafokonmu (Soul Discs)

Akrafokonmu were created by an artist of the Ashante people of west Africa. Neither the name of the artist nor the exact date these *akrafokonmu* were created are known. It is estimated that the pieces were made sometime during the beginning of the twentieth century, in or near the west African coastal region that has historically been called the Gold Coast. Today it is known as the nation of Ghana.

◀ **Artist unknown.** (Asante). *Akrafokonmu (Soul Discs).* Twentieth century.

Gold. Largest diameter: $4\frac{1}{2}$ inches (11.43 cm.). The Museum of Fine Arts, Houston, Texas.

About Art History

In the Asante culture, discs of various sizes are the most popular kind of jewelry and ornamentation. Gold beads, larger discs, and even larger pectorals are made by many Asante artists. In addition to being worn as jewelry these circular gold ornaments have been used to adorn ritual containers, stools, and weapons.

About the Artwork

A*krafokonmu* are ornamental breastplates or discs worn by a particular type of Ashante priest responsible for guarding and purifying a ruling chief's soul. These priests perform rituals for cleansing the chief's soul while wearing the akrafokonmu, serving as a representation of the soul. A white plant-fiber cord laced through the two holes at the top of the disc was tied around the wearer's neck to support the weight of the disc. The symbols pressed or pounded onto the surface of the *akrafokonmu* include fern leaves, symbolic of courage; cowrie shells, symbolic of wealth and fertility; and the larva of palm beetles, a delicacy eaten by the Ashante. Together these symbols create a message of hope for wealth, prosperity, and peace in the future.

About the Media

As the name Gold Coast implies, the soils of the coastal region of west Africa where these *akrafokonmu* were made were rich in elemental gold. Residents of the area developed impressive techniques for harvesting and processing the gold for use in the creation of beautiful artifacts, jewelry, and amulets. These *akrafokonmu* are made entirely of gold and small bits of metal solder that were used in their construction.

About the Technique

Each *akrafokonmu* is made from a solid gold sheet that was hammered and cut into shape. Solder was added where needed to secure smaller bits of gold for ornamentation. When the disc was being worn, a slender gold chain or plant-fiber cord would be strung through the small holes at its top.

UNIT 4 • Lesson 4

Artist Profile

Armor of George Clifford, Third Earl of Cumberland

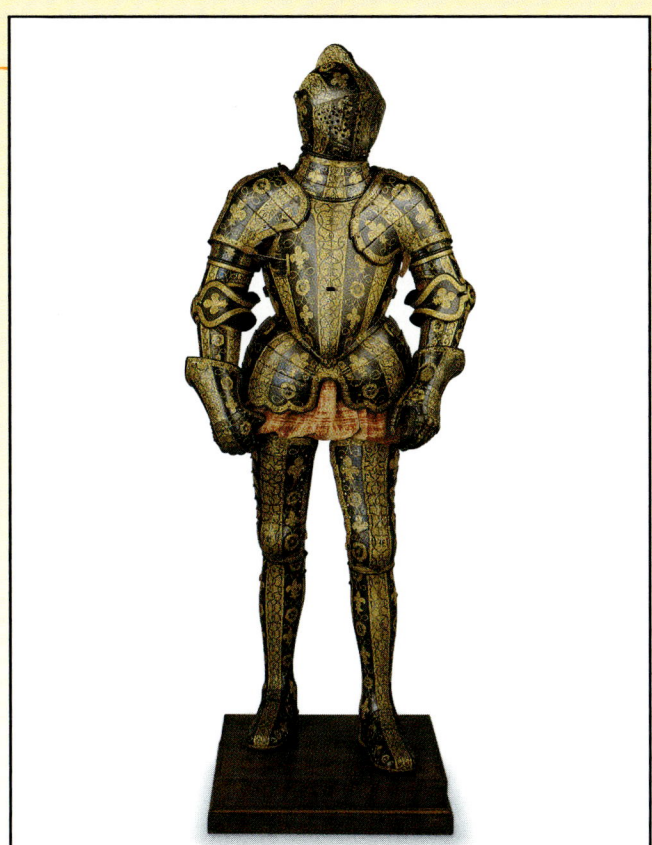

The *Armor of George Clifford, Third Earl of Cumberland* was made by artists and craftsmen of the Royal Workshops at Greenwich, England. The master armorer at that time, Jacob Halder, directed the creation of the opulent suit of armor. Pen and ink drawings of the complete work were included in a book called the *Jacob Album*, an illustrated record of the more spectacularly decorated suits of armor made at the Royal Workshops.

◀ **Royal Workshops.** (England). *Armor of George Clifford, Third Earl of Cumberland.* c. 1580–1585.

Steel, etched, blued, and gilded. 69 inches tall (176.53 cm.). The Metropolitan Museum of Art, New York, New York.

About Art History

George Clifford was an English nobleman who lived from 1558 to 1605. He was a favorite of Queen Elizabeth I and became Queen's Champion in 1590. Two years later he received the honor of being made a Knight of the Garter. George Clifford is most famous for capturing the Spanish fort in San Juan, Puerto Rico, in 1598.

About the Artwork

This armor is an ornate, decorative suit, atypical of the types of armor worn by common soldiers of the time. The Earl of Cumberland would have worn this suit during field games and tournaments, where beautiful special occasion armor would have been appropriate. The surface of the armor is covered in decorative metal etching and gold leaf. The craftmanship and materials with which it was created made this suit of armor costly and valuable. This suit looks more like a spectacular costume or work of art than a functional suit of protective battle wear, but it was worn for tournament fighting. The joints and hinges of the suit allowed a broad range of movement for the wearer.

About the Media

The *Armor of George Clifford, Third Earl of Cumberland* is made of etched steel and gold leaf.

Artist Profile

Bull's Eye Quilt

A label sewn onto the back of this quilt bears the name Alverda Herb, of the Herb family of Berks County, Pennsylvania. Fabrics identical to those used to make this quilt were used in the construction of similar quilts still in the possession of relatives of the Herb family.

◀ Attributed to **Alverda Herb.** (American). *Bull's Eye Quilt.* c. 1900–1920.

Cotton. 84½ × 86 inches (214.63 × 218.44 cm.). American Folk Art Museum, New York City, New York.

About Art History

Artists of the late nineteenth century and early twentieth century were fascinated with intricate patterns that formed optical illusions.

About the Artwork

This quilt was probably made to fulfill the utilitarian purpose of a bedspread. The design and pattern of this quilt might have been a product of its maker's imagination, might have been copied from an existing quilt, or might have come from a mail-order pattern or a pattern published in one of several ladies' magazines popular at the time.

About the Media

This quilt was made from many small pieces of colored cotton fabric and was sewn with cotton thread. Because cotton is durable and stands up well to repeated launderings, it does not decay as quickly as other quilting media such as silk and velvet. Most of the quilts remaining from the turn of the twentieth century are those made of cotton.

About the Technique

The construction of a quilt such as the one shown here begins with the collection of many small scraps and cuttings of fabric. These scraps are cut and will become the quilt's top layer. When the top layer stitching is complete, a bottom layer is sewn to the top, with batting, fiber filling, or feathers sewn into the middle layers. The finish stitching keeps the stuffing from shifting within the finished quilt.

Artist Profile

Carved Animals

These wooden sculptures were made by an unknown Zapotec artist from the Mexican state of Oaxaca. Although most residents of the Oaxaca Valley are farmers, many people carve animals and other small figures to sell to supplement their incomes. Oaxaca is a poor region and making a living there can be quite a struggle. Having a way to bring in extra money is very important to these farming families, and the sale of these popular wooden souvenirs has helped during times of economic need.

▲ **Artist unknown.** (Mexico). *Carved Animals.*
Private Collection.

About Art History

Wood carving has been an important part of Zapotec culture for hundreds of years. Designs and carving techniques have been passed down through many generations of Zapotec families.

About the Artwork

Small, hand-carved wooden figures from Oaxaca are also called *Alebrijes*. Most of these are made in the forms of wild and domestic animals, imaginary beasts, humans, and angels.

About the Media

These animals were carved from the soft wood of the copal tree, a species native to southern Mexico.

About the Technique

After they were hand-carved using machetes and small pocketknives, these animals were carefully sanded to a smooth finish. Their surfaces were then wiped clean of dust and painted using bright colors. Finishing touches such as facial features, patterns, and other small details were added by hand in a second layer of paint. Once dry, the wooden sculptures were ready to be displayed and sold.

Artist Profile

Ceremonial Hanging

▲ **Artist unknown.** (Indonesia). *Ceremonial Hanging.* c. 1900.

Cotton and metal wrapped yarns. $24\frac{3}{4} \times 95\frac{3}{4}$ inches (61.6 × 243.2 cm.). Dallas Museum of Art, Dallas, Texas.

This ceremonial hanging, also called a *palepai*, was crafted by an unknown Indonesian artist, probably a native of the Lampang province of the island Sumatra. Indonesia is a republic made up of more than 13,000 islands situated between the Pacific Ocean, the Indian Ocean, and the South China Sea. Indonesia is a densely populated nation made up of many different cultures and ethnic groups.

About Art History

Indonesia is made up of small and medium-sized islands, many of which have their own languages, religious beliefs, social structures, art forms, and styles of dress. Woven, handmade textiles have been an important art form throughout Indonesia for thousands of years. Not only did the more elaborate textiles represent the wealth and prosperity of their owners, the symbols and patterns of the weavings themselves have historically been a form of communication used by some ancient Indonesian cultures.

About the Artwork

This ceremonial hanging is a long woven, rectangular cloth. Images and figures embroidered onto the cloth include a large ship with multiple prows, trees, and animals with riders. Each of these images is symbolic and representational in Lampung society. The ship may be a symbol of spiritual transition in the face of crises or difficulties in life. The trees may represent the Tree of Life. Ceremonial cloths such as the one shown here were used by members of Lampung aristocracy during celebrations and rituals of importance, such as during weddings, funerals, and naming ceremonies for infants.

About the Media

Cotton cloth and metal-wrapped cotton yarn were used to make this ceremonial hanging.

About the Technique

Natives of Sumatra and other Indonesian islands developed their own unique styles of weaving and adorning cloth for use as clothing for ceremonial purposes. Ceremonial cloths made in Sumatra's Lampung province are among the most intricate, elaborately patterned and richly embroidered textiles in all of Indonesia.

Artist Profile

Ceremonial Skirt

This skirt, also called a *tapis,* was crafted by an unknown Indonesian artist. Indonesia is a republic of more than 13,000 islands situated between the Pacific Ocean, the Indian Ocean, and the South China Sea. Indonesia is a densely populated nation of many different cultures and ethnic groups. While the capital city of Jakarta has some of the tallest, most spectacular high-rise buildings and advanced technologies in the world, there are other areas where primitive rain forest-dwelling peoples live much like their ancestors have for centuries.

◀ **Artist unknown.** (Flores/Indonesian). *Ceremonial Skirt.* Nineteenth century.

Cotton, glass beads, shell, and metal. $68\frac{1}{2} \times 31\frac{1}{4}$ inches (173.99 × 79.38 cm.). Dallas Museum of Art, Dallas, Texas.

About Art History

Indonesia is made up of several islands, many of which have their own languages, religious beliefs, social structures, art forms, and styles of dress. Woven, handmade textiles have been an important art form throughout Indonesia for thousands of years. Not only did the more elaborate textiles represent the wealth and prosperity of their owners, the symbols and patterns of the weavings themselves were a form of communication used by some ancient Indonesian cultures.

About the Artwork

This tapis is a long, close-fitting, straight skirt that is wrapped around the lower body and either tucked in at the waist or secured by a cord or pin. In many parts of the world, they are worn by both women and men. This particular tapis was made to be worn during special occasions such as marriage ceremonies, funeral services, or the celebration of the birth of a child.

About the Media

Cotton cloth, glass beads, and embroidery thread were used to make this ceremonial skirt.

About the Technique

The black, woven cloth of this ceremonial skirt is decorated with elaborate embroidery and beadwork. Glass beads were sewn onto the special clothing of the wealthy, socially important members of Indonesian communities. The beadwork images include human figures, a boat, and spiders.

Artist Profile

Coming of Age Hat

This hat was made in China sometime during the twentieth century. The identity of the artist or artists who designed, sewed, and skillfully embroidered this spectacular hat is not known, but it is a typical example of the Coming-of-Age hats created in the twentieth century.

◀ **Artist unknown.** (Chinese).
Coming of Age Hat. Twentieth century.

Mixed media, embroidery. 12 × 15 inches (30.48 × 38.1 cm.). Private Collection.

About Art History

In China, young boys and their families celebrate a "coming of age" ceremony to mark the passing of a boy from childhood into the beginning of adulthood. This ceremony takes place when the boy is about twelve or thirteen years old—a time when he is expected to accept the responsibilities of becoming an adult. As part of the lavish celebration, the young man wears a special coming-of-age hat that has been made especially for him, such as the one shown here.

About the Artwork

This hat is adorned with intricate embroidered images, including a portrait of the boy for whom it was made. Symbols on the hat are meant to convey wishes for prosperity, luck, and long life. Ornate patterns of beadwork and silken tassels add to the magnificent, festive appearance of the hat.

About the Media

This hat is made of silk embroidery thread, glass beads, and cloth. The cloth that was used may have been silk, which has long been produced and used by Chinese craftspeople to create elegant and beautiful hats, shoes, robes, and other garments.

About the Technique

This hat was embroidered with silk. Silk embroidery is practiced throughout almost all of China. The provinces with the greatest production of silk embroidery are Jiangsu, Hunan, Sichuan, and Guangdong.

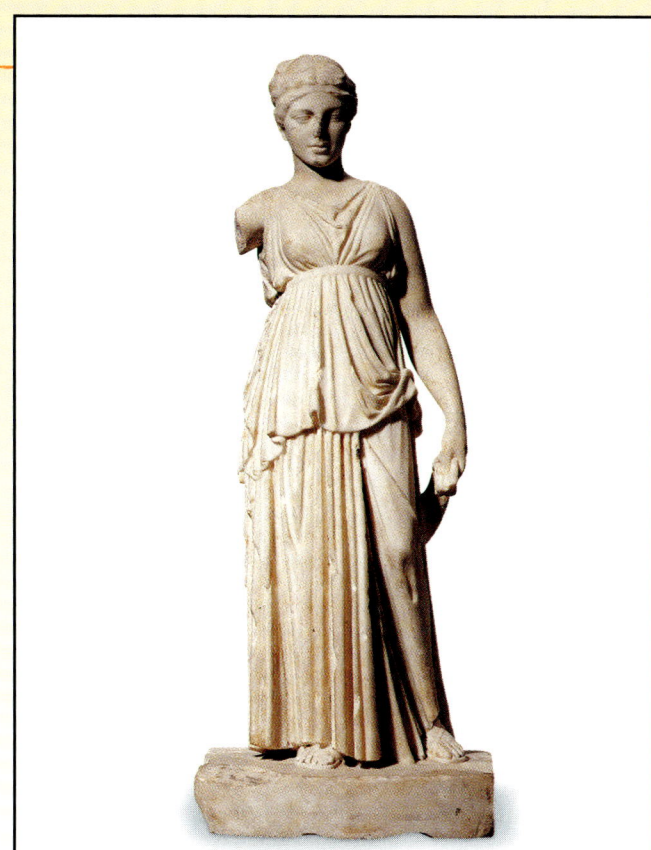

Artist Profile

Dancing Lady

This dancing lady sculpture was created by an unknown Greek sculptor sometime during the 1st century, B.C. The time period between the years 320 B.C. and 30 B.C. is known as the *Hellenistic* period of Greek history. The artist who created this sculpture must have subscribed to the classical style of sculpture practiced by artists of the fourth century B.C. This style was characterized by attention to detail and proportions considered to be the ideal of the human figure. Sculptors of the Hellenistic period often portrayed everyday subjects rather than the more mythological and heroic figures sculpted by artists of previous periods.

◀ **Artist unknown.** (Greece). *Dancing Lady*. c. 50 B.C.

Marble. $33\frac{5}{8}$ inches tall including base (85.4 cm.). The Cleveland Museum of Art, Cleveland, Ohio.

About Art History

In ancient Greece, visual artists were often writers, poets, philosophers, astronomers, and mathematicians as well. They considered it important to master many forms of artistic expression instead of focusing their energies in one area. Proportion was a main concern of sculptors and painters in ancient Greece, and artists devised what they considered the classic, perfectly proportioned human figure.

About the Artwork

This sculpture statue is a proportional, detailed portrait of a young Greek woman. Although the sculpture has been damaged over time, the position of the remaining portion of the right arm suggests that the original arm was somewhat raised, probably in a graceful pose befitting a dancer in motion. The positions of the figure's feet and left leg also suggest movement.

About the Media

This sculpture was carved from marble. A high level of skill was needed for a sculptor to achieve the smooth surface displayed in this piece.

About the Technique

The artist who sculpted this dancing lady used sharp chisels and other hand tools to carve and smooth the surface of the marble. The artists probably used a live model to begin the sculpture, but the details of her face and clothing probably came from the artist's own imagination. Sculptors in ancient Greece sometimes used models only as guidelines for the basic form of their work, not for copying the small details of the model's appearance.

Artist Profile

Egungun from Ogbomoso

This costume probably was made over many years by the members of a Yoruban family of west Africa. Because the cloth used to make the costume shows little sign of deterioration or age, it is assumed to have been made during the twentieth century. The majority of Yoruban people today live in the west African countries of Nigeria and Benin.

◀ **Artist unknown.** (Yoruban). *Egungun from Ogbomoso.* Twentieth century.

Cloth, wood, buttons. Approximately 60 inches (152.4 cm.). North Carolina Museum of Art, Raleigh, North Carolina.

About Art History

Ancient and contemporary Yoruban artwork is made using many different forms, styles, and media. Pottery, textiles, weaving, beadwork, metalwork, masks, and wooden carvings are some of the types of art for which the Yoruba are known. Yoruban works of art often have spiritual significance because the culture is heavily influenced by the belief in an afterworld where ancestors live and continue to affect the lives of their descendants on Earth. Effigies and other symbols representing the deceased are still honored and displayed in Yoruban homes today.

About the Artwork

This costume is actually just one part of a larger, more elaborate costume worn during a ritual ceremony honoring ancestors. The portion shown here is meant to hang down over the body. Strips of cloth are attached to a wooden frame located at the top, inside part of the costume. This is placed over the wearer's head. Amidst the drumming and singing of the Egungun ceremony, a dancer wearing this costume whirls around in the center of a group of spectators. As the dancer spins, the many strips of cloth fan outward in a circle, brushing against the people in the group. The moving air created by this spinning is said to be the blessings of the ancestors upon those watching.

About the Media

This costume is made of wood, buttons, and strips of many different types of colorful, patterned cloth.

About the Technique

After the costume's wooden top frame is constructed, the strips and panels of patterned cloth are added a few at a time by the members of a family. Traditionally the family member who wears the Egungun costume and acts as the dancer during a year's ceremony is the one who adds the strips of cloth for that year. These pieces of cloth are valuable. After many years of ceremonies, an Egungun costume like the one shown here may become heavy with many layers of cloth.

Artist Profile

Face Jugs

These face jugs were made by an unknown artist or artists sometime during the twentieth century. Face jug pottery is a traditional art form from the American South and the Appalachian Mountains. Because face jugs have been made in thousands of American communities for nearly two hundred years, it is often difficult to find information about the individual creator of a particular piece.

▲ **Artist unknown.** (United States). *Face Jugs.*
c. Twentieth century.

Earthenware. Private collection.

About Art History

The first face jug known to have been made in North America was created by a Massachusetts potter in 1810. Before long the art form had become quite popular in the South. A porcelain factory in Bath, South Carolina, began making large quantities of face jugs in the mid-nineteenth century, and the tradition soon spread to North Carolina and Georgia. There has been a renewed interest in face jug pottery, and sculptures based on face jugs are currently made by artists all over the United States.

About the Artwork

Face jugs, also called *ugly jugs,* have been made in different forms and with different materials over the years. Traditionally face jugs were sculpted from locally available clay soils and finished with homemade mineral glazes. Although the original purpose of these strange-looking jugs is not known, it is clear that many who purchased them used them to store liquor. It was believed that a scary, monstrous face on a jug would frighten children away from it, thus protecting the alcoholic contents from curious youngsters. The more gruesome or ugly the face, the more repellant the jug would be to a child.

About the Media

Various types of clay have been used to make face jugs. Whatever was most readily available to potters was used to make their ceramic and stoneware jugs.

About the Technique

Face jugs have been made using many different methods. The easiest methods are begun by making pinch pots or coiled ropes of clay to form the basic structure of the jug. Once the jug begins to take shape, the face, ears, and other details can be carved or added. Once the sculpting of a jug is complete, it is dried, glazed or painted, and fired in a kiln.

Artist Profile

Face Mask of `Kumugwe'

This mask was carved and painted by an unknown artist of the Kwakwaka'wakw (or Kwakiutl, as they are also known) peoples of northwestern Canada. The term *Kwakiutl* is used to refer collectively to approximately 5,500 tribes of the Canadian First Nations, while *Kwakwaka'wakw* is used by the Kwakiutl people to describe themselves and their tribal affiliations with other members of the Kwakiutl.

◀ **Artist unknown (Kwakwaka'wakw).** (Canada). *Face Mask of `Kumugwe'.* c. 1880.

Alder, red cedar bark, cloth, paint.
$19\frac{1}{4} \times 17 \times 6$ inches (48.9 × 43.18 × 15.24 cm.).
Hauberg Collection, Seattle Museum of Art, Seattle, Washington.

About Art History

Masks such as this one have been worn during Kwakiutl ceremonies, dances, theatrical performances, and heritage celebrations for centuries. Beautiful, bizarre, and sometimes gruesome masks representing sea creatures, sky beings, forest and mountain beings, and animal spirits are still made and worn by Kwakiutl people today.

About the Artwork

This ceremonial mask is meant to represent the chief of the undersea creatures, an important character from Kwakwaka'wakw mythology. This mask was worn by a dancer in an important social event called a *potlatch. Potlatch* celebrations, which usually include one or more days of feasting, dancing, singing, and traditional storytelling, are still an important part of the cultures of Native American tribal groups in western Canada and the northwestern United States.

About the Media

This mask was made from alder wood, red cedar bark, cloth, and enamel paint. Traditionally, paints were mixed in a few basic colors, and were used to enhance or emphasize the carved features on the mask. Enamel paints were not used on these masks until the twentieth century, so the use of enamels here is a good indication that this mask was repainted during the twentieth century.

About the Technique

This mask was carved from alder wood and was adorned with frayed strips of cedar bark. The mask was then painted using traditional colors of red, blue, black, and white. Traditional masks from western Canada feature deep, arching grooves, and geometric and organic shapes, with both convex and concave curves sculpted into their surfaces, which give the masks exaggerated facial features and expressions.

Artist Profile

King's Crown

This crown was made by an unknown artist of the Yoruban culture of west Africa. Yoruba-speaking people are among the most numerous in Africa, with an estimated population of more than 25 million today. They live in Benin and Nigeria. Yoruban artisans are experts at creating pottery and in weaving, beadworking, and metalsmithing.

◀ **Artist unknown.** (Yoruba). *King's Crown.* c. 1930.
Bamboo framework, beads, cloth, leather.
12 inches diameter (30.48 cm.).
Saint Louis Museum of Art, Saint Louis, Missouri.

About Art History

The crown is a beautifully ornate example of a type of Yoruban ceremonial headdress called *adenla*. Adenlas have been worn traditionally by members of Yoruban royalty during rites of passage.

About the Artwork

This *adenla* has a brimless, conical shape and is adorned with intricate beadwork and colorful thread. It is estimated that this crown was created around the year 1930. One of the many interesting features of this crown is the figure of a bird at its top peak. Birds, especially woodpeckers, are featured on some *adenlas* as symbols of the Yoruban social ranking system, or pecking order.

The beaded fringe surrounding the bottom of the headdress hangs in long strands, meant to shield the royal wearer from the distractions of the outside world. This enables him to focus inwardly on the needs of his people and his responsibilities as a leader.

About the Media

This crown was constructed using cloth and beads over a bamboo framework.

> Artist Profile

Quilt

This American quilt was made in upstate New York during the late 1800s. Although it is not known who created the quilt, it may be assumed that the artist was a woman, or several women, from a relatively prosperous American family. During the Victorian era when this quilt was made, nearly all quiltmakers were women. Considering the amount of time needed to design, cut, assemble, and sew a quilt, the maker would have to be someone who had significant time to spend on these tasks, free from other work. The quilt may have been made by a group of women, perhaps at a quilting bee or quilting party, but the process would still have been time-consuming.

◀ **Artist unknown.** (American) *Quilt.* c. 1885.

Pieced and embroidered silk, velvet, velveteen, and cotton sateen. $69\frac{1}{4} \times 68\frac{1}{4}$ inches. Museum of International Folk Art, Santa Fe, New Mexico.

About Art History

Artists of the late nineteenth century were fascinated with intricate geometric designs and patterns that formed optical illusions. The circular, fan-type design featured on this quilt probably was inspired by looking through a kaleidoscope, which was a popular toy during this time period.

About the Artwork

Quilts featuring elaborate designs and beautiful stitching and embroidery were often made as wedding gifts, baby gifts, or as "friendship quilts" to be given to friends or family as an heirloom in the event of their relocation to a new area.

About the Media

This quilt was made from many small pieces of colored silk, velvet, velveteen, and cotton fabric and was sewn with cotton thread.

About the Technique

Patchwork quilts are all assembled in a similar way, although an infinite number of patterns, designs, styles, and sewing techniques are used to create individual quilts. When the quilt design and pattern have been decided upon these scraps are cut into the desired shapes, then stitched together from what will become the underside of the quilt's top layer. When the top layer stitching is complete, a bottom layer is sewn to the top, with batting, fiber filling, or feathers sewn into the middle layers. Finish stitching is typically added from the outside as a way to keep the stuffing or layers of material from shifting within the finished quilt. Top-stitching patterns can be quite intricate and decorative.

Artist Profile

United States Capitol

In 1792 a competition was held to decide who would design and build the United States Capitol building. The winner of this competition was amateur architect Dr. William Thornton. Thornton devised a plan for a central rotunda with north wings off to its sides that would house the Senate and the House of Representatives. When building began in 1793, President George Washington laid the cornerstone. Construction of the United States Capitol was completed 1830.

◀ *United States Capitol.* 1793–1830; 1851–1863.

Stone-bearing masonry and cast-iron dome. Washington, D.C.

About Art History

In November of 1800, the United States Congress met in the Capitol building for the first time. The building was still under construction at that time, and would not be completed for another 30 years due to several setbacks. The most notable and devastating setback occurred during the War of 1812 when the Capitol was burned and almost destroyed by soldiers of the British Army. Architect Benjamin Latrobe began the reconstruction in 1815 but was replaced by Boston native Charles Bulfinch in 1818. Bulfinch directed the completion of the Capitol in 1826. Before dust from the construction had settled, a decision was made that the Capitol was too small for the needs of Congress. The original building was extended, and a much larger Capitol building was completed in 1851.

About the Artwork

An enormous, sprawling building, the Capitol has 540 rooms. Its dome measures 96 feet in diameter and has 108 windows.

About the Media

The original Capitol building, built in the late eighteenth and early nineteenth centuries, was constructed of sandstone. Later additions to the building were done in white marble and cast iron. The huge dome of the Capitol, designed by Thomas Walter, is made entirely of cast iron.

About the Technique

Although the original Capitol building was designed in the dignified and sedate style of neoclassical architecture, it was partially redesigned in the more grand and decorative Victorian style popular when the building was extended. Sculptors and painters were commissioned to decorate rooms within the Capitol, and over the next 25 years the walls and ceilings of the corridors, committee rooms, rotunda, and the lobby were adorned with fresco paintings.

Artist Profile

Woman's Headcloth

This headcloth was made by an unidentified Mayan artist from Chichicastenango, located in the highlands of Guatemala. Art historians estimate that the piece was made between 1935 and 1945. The Mayan people, founders of a vast, powerful, and ancient kingdom, have historically lived throughout an enormous geographic area of what is today Mexico and Central America.

◀ **Artist Unknown.** (Guatemala). *Woman's Headcloth.* c. 1935–1945.

Cotton, silk, and wool. 50 × 44 inches. (127 × 111.8 cm.). Dallas Museum of Art, Dallas, Texas.

About Art History

Chichicastenango is famous for producing handwoven textiles. Although Mayan people from both Central and South American locations create beautiful cloth and works of textile art, the Maya of the Guatemalan highlands have a unique style of weaving. The cloth shown here was made using the same method of weaving practiced by the Chichicastenango Maya for generations. Historians can date evidence of the Mayan culture to 700 B.C.

About the Artwork

This headcloth or carrying cloth was made to serve as either a sling for carrying a baby or as a sunshade, which would have been folded into a square and worn atop the head. The images and symbols embroidered onto this cloth include deer and other animals, women wearing triangular skirts, double-headed birds, and large plants or trees. The decoration of this cloth was planned and created according to an individual's personal tastes. It is not known whether the wearer of this cloth was also its designer and maker, or whether the piece was made by an artist and then given or sold to the wearer.

About the Media

This headcloth or carrying cloth was made from cotton, silk, and wool fibers.

About the Technique

During the past 100 years, textiles from the Guatemalan highlands have often featured symmetrical patterns of geometric shapes, zigzag lines, and floral designs. As seen in this headcloth or carrying cloth, these textiles also display the creativity of their creators.